Glasgow

Alan Murphy & Nick Bruno

Credits

Footprint credits

Editorial: Jo Williams
Production and layout: Emma Bryers
Maps: Kevin Feeney
Cover: Pepi Bluck

Publisher: Patrick Dawson
Managing Editor: Felicity Laughton
Advertising: Elizabeth Taylor
Sales and marketing: Kirsty Holmes

Photography credits

Front cover: Gordon Saunders/
Shutterstock.com
Back cover: CraigBurrows/Shutterstock.com

Printed in Great Britain by CPI Antony Rowe,
Chippenham, Wiltshire

Every effort has been made to ensure that
the facts in this guidebook are accurate.
However, travellers should still obtain advice
from consulates, airlines, etc, about travel
and visa requirements before travelling.
The authors and publishers cannot accept
responsibility for any loss, injury or
inconvenience however caused.

Contains Ordnance Survey data
© Crown copyright and database
right 2013

Publishing information

Footprint *Focus Glasgow*
1st edition
© Footprint Handbooks Ltd
June 2013

ISBN: 978 1 909268 23 4
CIP DATA: A catalogue record for this book
is available from the British Library

® Footprint Handbooks and the Footprint
mark are a registered trademark of
Footprint Handbooks Ltd

Published by Footprint
6 Riverside Court
Lower Bristol Road
Bath BA2 3DZ, UK
T +44 (0)1225 469141
F +44 (0)1225 469461
footprinttravelguides.com

Distributed in the USA by Globe Pequot
Press, Guilford, Connecticut

The content of Footprint *Focus Glasgow*
has been taken directly from Footprint's
Scotland Handbook, which was researched
and written by Alan Murphy.

Contents

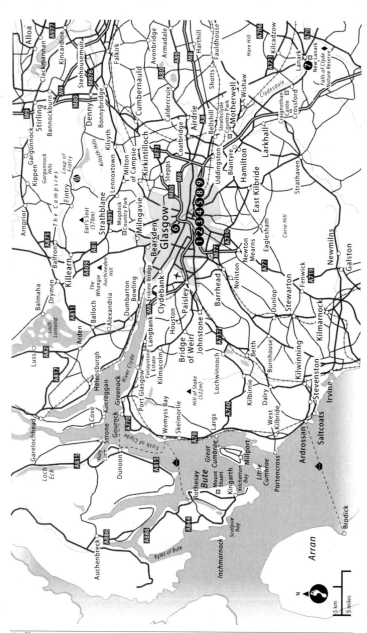

There's an old saying that Edinburgh is the capital but Glasgow has the capital. This dates back to the late 19th century, when Glasgow was the 'Second City of the Empire'. It was a thriving, cultivated city grown rich on the profits from its cotton mills, coal mines and shipyards. The heavy industries have long gone, but Glasgow has lost none of its energy and excitement, and its people possess a style and swagger that makes their Edinburgh counterparts look staid and stuffy by comparison. Just take a stroll round the revived Merchant City or along Byres Road in the West End and you'll witness a degree of posing that is Continental in its fervency. The licensing laws may not be Continental but they're more liberal than London and the atmosphere is infused with those vital Glasgow ingredients missing from so many large British cities – warmth and humour. Perhaps that's because it doesn't feel British. Glasgow is often described as European; for the diversity of its architecture, accessibility of its art and optimism of its people. It's also compared with North America; for its gridiron streets and its wisecracking streetwise citizens.

It's no accident that Glasgow has been chosen as European City of Culture, UK City of Architecture and Design and to host the Turner Prize for contemporary art. Its vibrant cultural scene stages many world-class events and festivals. Selection as the 2014 Commonwealth Games host means even more culture with cosmopolitan flavours. Alongside some medieval churches Glasgow's architectural bedrock lays in its magnificent Victorian buildings. Sir John Betjeman, Poet Laureate and architectural enthusiast, described Glasgow as the "greatest Victorian city in Europe". In recent years the Merchant City's commercial palaces have been transformed into stylish centres for shopping, eating, the arts and socializing. The River Clyde now looks more welcoming with its futuristic, glass and steel 'starchitecture', most recently Zaha Hadid's Riverside Museum. The Clydeside Walkway is an attempt to direct Glasgow's great river towards a post-industrial future of leisure and tourism.

Planning your trip

Best time to visit Glasgow

Despite the Gulf Stream warming the West Coast of Scotland, you can rely on the weather being inconsistent at all times of the year in Glasgow. Winters are generally mild with more rain than snow, though sub-zero temperatures and prolonged cold snaps have been known. Summers do provide some days of sunshine, with temperatures of up to 25°C (77°F). Prevailing westerly winds from the Atlantic bring rain showers. The weather is unpredictable – so morning sun can be followed by rain, sleet and even snow. So be prepared at all times of the year for any eventuality. Mid-May to late August are the best months for a chance of warmer weather and sunshine.

Where to go in Glasgow

A weekend and more

A weekend provides ample time to see Glasgow's main attractions and sample its shopping, eating and nightlife. A good place to start is near **Queen Street Station** at George Square, the grand Victorian public space. Visit the opulent **City Chambers** to get a feel for the civic pride, wealth and confidence of the city when it opened in 1888. On Queen Street head to the Wellington equestrian statue and the former residence of a tobacco baron, now the home of **Gallery of Modern Art** (**GoMA**), which exhibits contemporary art in impressive surroundings. **Buchanan Street** and **Princes Square** provide lots of shopping options and a taster of Rennie Mackintosh design at **Willow Tea Rooms**. The gridiron layout of **Merchant City** and its recast tobacco warehouses offer impressive architecture, independent shopping and some of the smartest eateries in town. **Trades Hall**, **City Halls** and **Italian Centre** are places to discover the city's 14 traditional trades, high-brow cultural capital and today's European-influenced café and fashion culture. For those after more left-field attractions, head to **Trongate 103** arts hub and the quirky shops and galleries around King Steet and towards the Clyde. Heading east along Gallowgate brings you closer to the city's working class past and present: the market characters of the **Barras**, **Glasgow Green**, the **Winter Gardens** and the **People's Palace**. Travel back to Glasgow's medieval past from Mercat Cross up High Street to **Glasgow Cathedral**, **Provand's Lordship** and the **Necropolis**.

Those who enjoy the arts and architecture should head to **Glasgow School of Art**, **The Lighthouse** and **CCA**. **Tenement House** provides an evocative snapshot of tenement life. Fit and keen walkers could go west passing the impressive building of St Vincent Street to Mitchell Street library.

The sights of leafy **West End** and new **Clydeside** developments should not be missed and can be enjoyed for those with stamina and more time. **Kelvingrove Park, Museum and Gallery**, the **Botanic Gardens** and **Riverside Museum** have open spaces for those seeking more leisurely sight seeing. Families should place these at the top of their must-see list of sights. The **Science Centre** is another child-friendly attraction. Couples and those after quirky shopping and nightlife should explore **Byres Road** and its cobbled lanes.

Many will want to prioritise a visit to the **Burrell Collection** and its artworks. A trip South Side can also provide lots of outdoor walks in the area's many green spaces, including **Pollok Country Park**.

Don't miss...

A week or more

A week or more provides ample time to visit the main sights in the City Centre, West End, South Side and explore places further afield. Themed tours and walks can be planned such as a Charles Rennie Macintosh tour of his architectural legacy across some eight sights from the **Lighthouse** and **GSA** to **Queen's Cross Church** and **House of an Art Lover**. Most of the Mackintosh sights are in and around the city centre, with the exception of **Hill House** in Helensburgh, and can be visited comfortably in two or three days. Lovers of fine buildings will also want to see some examples of Alexander 'Greek' Thomson, Glasgow's other great architect, especially **Holmwood House**, which has been described as a 'sonnet in stone'. The **Clyde Valley** has country parks, the **David Livingstone Centre** and fascinating mills of **New Lanark**. Across the water to Bute is the wonderful **Mount Stuart** with its lush gardens and historic interiors. Outdoorsy types could venture north to the shores of **Loch Lomond** or beyond to the **Trossachs** and **Highlands**.

Getting to Glasgow

Air

There are flights to Glasgow International Airport (GLA) from many European cities – and direct flights from North America – to Glasgow. For more options there are many connections via London. **British Airways** has many services from London's airports and UK airports from Jersey to Shetland. Of the budget airlines, **easyJet** offers the most civilized service and many UK options, with services from Amsterdam, Belfast, Berlin, Bristol, London and Paris. Rundown Glasgow Prestwick (PIK) hosts low cost operator **Ryanair** flights from Ireland and Europe.

Glasgow International Airport ⓘ *T0141-842 7607/0844-481 5555, www.baa.co.uk/ glasgow*, is 8 miles west of the city, at junction 28 on the M8. It handles domestic and international flights. Terminal facilities include car hire, bank ATMs, currency exchange, left luggage, tourist information, T0141-8484440, and shops, restaurants and bars. To get into town take a **Glasgow Airport Link** bus from outside Arrivals. They leave every 10-15 minutes to Buchanan bus station, with drop-off points at Central and Queen Street train stations; 25-30 minutes, £3.30 single, £5 return. Tickets can be bought from the driver. Buses to the airport leave from Buchanan Street bus station and stop outside the main TIC (see below). A taxi from the airport to the city centre costs around £20.

Glasgow Prestwick ① *T01292-511000, www.gpia.co.uk*, is 30 miles southwest of the city. It is used by **Ryanair** from London Stansted, also for flights from Paris Beauvais, Dublin, Frankfurt Hahn, Stockholm and Brussels. Trains to and from Central Station leave every 30 minutes (taking 45 minutes; £2.50 single if you show your Ryanair ticket, or £5). The taxi fare is around £60.

Bus

All long-distance buses to and from Glasgow arrive and depart from Buchanan Bus station, on Killermont Street, T0141-332 7133, three blocks north of George Square. A number of companies offer express coach services day and night around the country and to most English cities; these include **Citylink Coaches** ① *T08705-505050, www.citylink.co.uk*, and **National Express** ① *T08705-808080, www.nationalexpress.com*.

Rail

Glasgow has two main train stations: Central Station is the terminus for all trains to southern Scotland, England and Wales; and Queen Street serves the north and east of Scotland. A shuttle bus runs every 10 minutes between Central Station (Gordon Street entrance) and Queen Street, at the corner of George Square. It takes 10 minutes to walk between the two. For information on rail services and fares, call **National Rail Enquiries** ① *T08457-484950 (advance credit/debit card bookings T08457-550033)*.

Transport in Glasgow

The best way to get around the city centre sights is by walking, although some of the hills are very steep. If you want to explore the West End or South Side, you'll need to use the public transport – which is generally good, efficient and reasonably priced – or taxis. See also Transport, page 83.

Bus

Buses in the city are run by **First Glasgow** and use white buses with a pink stripe. **Arriva** operate buses linking the city centre to Paisley and Braehead and use white and green buses. The frequency of bus services depends on the route, but generally speaking buses run every 10-15 minutes on most main routes Monday to Friday 0700-1900. Outside these peak times services vary so it's best to check timetables with **Traveline Scotland** ① *T0870-608 2608*. The areas around Queen Street and Central stations are the city's main transport hubs. There's a useful bus map of the city, mapmate, produced by First Glasgow available from SPT travel outlets, the TIC and various shops in the city, price £1.

Road and taxi

It is relatively easy to get around Glasgow by car, especially as the M8 runs right through the heart of the city. Parking is not a problem either. There are sufficient street meters and 24-hour multi-storey car parks dotted around the centre, at Buchanan Galleries, St Enoch Centre, Mitchell Street, Oswald Street, Waterloo Street and Cambridge Street. Taxis are plentiful and reasonably priced and can be hailed from anywhere in the city. There are taxi ranks at Central and Queen Street train stations and Buchanan bus station. Minimum fare around the city centre is £2.50. To the Burrell collection from the city centre should cost around £13.

Ticket to ride

There are some useful saver tickets available that can save you money and are very flexible.

FirstDay Tourist ticket allows visitors to hop on and off any First bus in Glasgow all day, before 1000 it's £2.50, after £2.20.

Roundabout Glasgow ticket covers all Underground and train transport in the city for one day and costs £4. Valid Monday to Friday after 0900 and weekends.

Discovery ticket gives unlimited travel on the Underground for a day (valid after 0930 Monday to Friday and weekends). It costs £1.70.

Daytripper ticket gives unlimited travel on all transport networks throughout Glasgow, the Clyde coast and Clyde Valley. It' valid for one day and costs £8 for one adult and two children, or £14 for two adults and up to four children.

Subway

The best way to get from the city centre to the West End is to use the city's Underground, or subway as it's also known, whose stations are marked with a huge orange 'U' sign. This is less effective for the South Side but for that there's a vast range of buses from the city centre. There's also an extensive suburban train network run by **SPT** ① *www.spt.co.uk*, which is a fast and efficient way to reach the suburbs south of the Clyde.

Bicycle

Glasgow city center traffic can be negotiated on bike with care and effort (there are some steep hills), while the leafy areas and parks of the West End and South Side are more pleasurable tracts to explore. For bike hire contact: **Billy Bilsland Cycles** ① *176 Saltmarket, T0141-552 0841, www.billybilslandcycles.co.uk*, or **Gear Bikes** ① *19 Gibson St, West End, T0141-339 1179, www.gearbikes.com*. Prices start at £15 for four hours or £20 for full-day hire on a hybrid bike. See also Cycling, page 82, for cycle routes in and around the city.

Where to stay in Glasgow

Glasgow has a good range of accommodation. Most of the hotels, guesthouses, B&Bs and hostels are in the city centre and the West End or south of the river, around Queen's Park. The best area to find good value mid-range accommodation is the West End, around Kelvingrove Park and the university. This is a good area to stay in, as it's convenient for several of the city's major sights as well as many of the best bars and restaurants. It provides a good balance of leafy outdoor space, less traffic and a concentration of the more interesting independent shops, bars and venues. For access to most of the shops and nightlife – and for avoiding taxi fares – look for accommodation in the city centre and Merchant City. Central Glasgow has some very stylish hotels and many self-catering apartment options these days. Glasgow has undergone something of a revolution on the hotel front in recent years and the market is highly competitive. A large number of big chains have opened up in the city, offering everything from deluxe accommodation to simple low cost lodging – meaning that there are often good deals available to travellers prepared to shop around. The city also has several boutique hotels, offering stylish accommodation with more character than the international chains. Finding a decent room for the night can be difficult during the major festivals and in July and August and it's best to book ahead. The tourist information centre can help find somewhere to stay and also publishes a free accommodation guide.

Price codes

Where to stay

££££ £160 and over   **£££** £90-160

££ £50-90   **£** under £50

Prices include taxes and service charge, but not meals. They are based on a double room in high season.

Restaurants

£££ over £30   **££** £15-30   **£** under £15

Prices quoted are for a two-course meal excluding drink or service charge.

Another alternative for longer stays and families/groups is renting self-catering accommodation. Although much of the serviced accommodation in the city is quite upmarket there are affordable options available in attractive areas.

A good option for those on a budget is campus accommodation. The universities open their halls of residence to visitors mainly during the summer vacation (late June to September) but some all year. Many rooms are basic and small, with shared bathrooms, but some are more comfortable with private bathrooms, twin and family units and self-contained apartments and shared houses. Full-board, half-board, B&B and self-catering options are all available. Prices for bed and breakfast tend to be roughly the same as for most B&Bs, but self-catering can be very economical. Local tourist offices have information on accommodation.

Food and drink in Glasgow

Forget the deep-fried Mars bar. OK, it was invented here – and is still available in some establishments – along with other Caledonian culinary delights like the deep-fried pizza, deep-fried black pudding and the deep-fried Cadbury's Creme Egg. These may be the headline grabbing foods that everyone associates with Glasgow, but they really don't reflect the quality and variety of food that the city has to offer. Glasgow has undergone a culinary renaissance and it continues unabated. Glasgow has always boasted a wide selection of ethnic eateries, particularly Indian, Chinese and Italian restaurants, and these have been joined by a growing number of cuisines from around the globe. Many of the immigrants that have made their home here – from Italians in the early 20th century to more recent Asian immigration – have created new hybrid cuisines. Second and third generation Italian-Scots keep traditions inherited from mainly Tuscan and Southern Italian families: combining them with tastes acquired from a Scots upbringing in the city's many Italian eateries. Scottish cuisine now reflects the growing trend of marrying traditional Scottish ingredients with continental and international flavours and styles. Meats like venison, pheasant, lamb and beef are often on the menu, and haggis may feature too – often as a starter so as not to frighten the uninitiated. Fresh local fish is also widely available. Look out for salmon, halibut, scallops, langoustines, mackerel and Loch Fyne kippers. Vegetarians are also well catered for. There are a handful of vegetarian or vegan restaurants, and most places now offer substantial and imaginative vegetarian options.

The greatest concentration of eating places is around Byres Road in the West End, which is heavily populated by students and therefore the best area for cheap but stylish places to eat. Merchant City contains most of the designer brasseries, which are more expensive. The city centre has the main share of pricey but superb restaurants. For those on a tight budget, many city restaurants offer cheap business lunches. Pre-theatre dinner menus also provide an opportunity to sample some of the finest food at affordable prices, if you don't mind eating before 1900. Many of the restaurants are open seven days a week.

Glasgow prides itself on its café society and many of the new, trendy designer cafés make it seem more like Barcelona or Greenwich Village than the west coast of Scotland. Glasgow is also full of authentic Italian cafés where you can enjoy a cheap fry-up, pasta dish or panino washed down with frothy cappuccino. Whatever your preference, you won't have any trouble finding the right place for that essential caffeine shot during a hard day's sightseeing or shopping. Glasgow is also the home of the tea-room and those who insist on their mid-afternoon infusion won't be disappointed. Most cafés also serve food and are often the most economical option for a midday snack or meal.

Festivals in Glasgow

Glasgow doesn't like to be overshadowed by Edinburgh, and has many notable festivals. For a list of upcoming festivals and other events consult www.visitscotland.com/see-do/events.

Mid-Jan to Feb Celtic Connections music festival features artists from around the world celebrating Celtic music traditional and contemporary. It is held in various venues with major nights at the Royal Concert Hall. T0141-353 8000, www.celticconnections.com.

Mid- to late Mar Glasgow Comedy Festival, T0141-552 2070, www.glasgow comedyfestival.com. Top acts from around the world do stand-up in many venues across the city.

Apr to May Glasgow International Festival of Visual Art, www.glasgowinternational.org. Biennial arts festival – that takes place in even number years – attracting international contemporary artists and is considered a cutting-edge alternative to the glitzy arts extravaganzas of Venice, New York and London.

Late May to Jun West End Festival, T0141-341 0844, www.westendfestival.co.uk. Glasgow's biggest festival brings parades, music and cultural events to the West End parks and venues.

Late Jun Glasgow International Jazz Festival, www.jazzfest.co.uk. Jazz concerts in intimate venues all over the city.

Mid-Aug World Pipe Band Championships, T0141-287 8985, www.theworlds.co.uk. Now in a 2-day format, staged at its traditional home on Glasgow Green.

Oct to Nov Glasgay, Britain's largest lesbian and gay arts festival established in 1993, held in various venues, T0141-552 7575, www.glasgay.co.uk. See also www.seeglasgow.com.

Essentials A-Z

Accident and emergency
For police, fire brigade, ambulance and, in certain areas, mountain rescue or coastguard, T999 or T112.

Disabled travellers
For travellers with disabilities, visiting Scotland independently can be a difficult business. While most theatres, cinemas, libraries and modern tourist attractions are accessible to wheelchairs, tours of many historic buildings and finding accommodation remains problematic. Many large, new hotels do have disabled suites, but far too many B&Bs, guesthouses and smaller hotels remain ill-equipped to accept bookings from people with disabilities. However, through the work of organizations such as **Disability Scotland** the Government is being pressed to further improve the Disability Discrimination Act and access to public amenities and transport. As a result, many buses and **FirstScotRail**'s train services now accommodate wheelchair-users whilst city taxis should carry wheelchair ramps.

Wheelchair users, and blind or partially sighted people are automatically given 30-50% discount on train fares, and those with other disabilities are eligible for the **Disabled Person's Railcard** (www.disabled persons-railcard.co.uk), which costs £20 per year and gives a third off most tickets. If you will need assistance at a railway station, call **FirstScotRail** before travelling on T0800-912 2901. There are no discounts on buses.

If you are disabled you should contact the travel officer of your national support organization. They can provide literature or put you in touch with travel agents specializing in tours for the disabled. **VisitScotland** produces a guide, *Accessible Scotland*, for disabled travellers, and many local tourist offices can provide accessibility details for their area. Alternatively, call its information hotline on T0845-859 1006.

Useful organizations include:
Capability Scotland, ASCS, 11 Ellersly Rd, Edinburgh EH12 6HY, T0131-337 9876, or Textphone 0131-346 2529, www.capability-scotland.org.uk,
Holiday Care Service, T0845-124 9971, www.holidaycare.org.uk, www.tourismforall. org.uk. Both websites are excellent sources of information about travel and for identifying accessible accommodation in the UK.
Royal Association for Disability and Rehabilitation (RADAR), Unit 12, City Forum, 250 City Rd, London EC1V 8AF, T020-7250 3222, www.radar.org.uk. A good source of advice and information. It produces the *National Key Scheme Guide* (£13.99) and distributes the Radar NKS key (from £4 including postage) for gaining access to over 9000 toilet facilities across the UK.

Driving
The UK drives on the left hand side of the road. To drive here, you require a current driving licence. A foreign licence is valid in the UK for up to 12 months. Drivers must be properly insured and it is advisable to check your policy prior to your journey. It is compulsory to wear seat belts in the front seat. If the vehicle has seat belts in the back, they must be worn too. For additional information on driving, maps and resources on travel insurance and road service, contact the RAC (**Royal Automobile Club**) www.rac.co.uk or The AA (**Automobile Association**) www.theaa.com. For up to date traffic and information on roadworks check www.trafficscotland.org and www.bbc. co.uk/travelnews.

Electricity
The current in Britain is 240V AC. Plugs have 3 square pins and adapters are widely available.

Gay and lesbian
Lesbian and Gay Switchboard,
T0141-847 0447, open daily 0700-2200.
Stonewall Scotland, LGBT Centre,
11 Dixon St, T0141-204 0746.

Health
No vaccinations are required for entry into
Britain. Citizens of EU countries are entitled
to free medical treatment at National Health
Service (NHS) hospitals on production of
a European Health Insurance Card (EHIC).
For details, see the **Department of Health**
website, www.dh.gov.uk/travellers. Also,
Australia, New Zealand and several other
non-EU European countries have reciprocal
healthcare arrangements with Britain.
Citizens of other countries will have to pay
for all medical services, except accident
and emergency care given at Accident and
Emergency (A&E) Units at most (but not all)
National Health Service hospitals. Health
insurance is therefore strongly advised for
citizens of non-EU countries.

Pharmacists can dispense only a
limited range of drugs without a doctor's
prescription. Most are open during normal
shop hours, though some are open late,
especially in larger towns. Local newspapers
will carry lists of which are open late.
Doctors' surgeries are usually open from
around 0830-0900 till 1730-1800, though
times vary. Outside surgery hours you can
go to the casualty department of the local
hospital for any complaint requiring urgent
attention. For the address of the nearest
hospital or doctors' surgery consult
www.nhs24.com or call T08454-242424.
See also individual town and city directories
throughout the book for details of local
medical services.

Insurance
Comprehensive travel (and medical)
insurance is strongly recommended for all
travellers. You should check any exclusions
and ensure that your policy covers you for
all the activities you want to undertake.

Keep details of your insurance documents
separately. Scanning them, then emailing
yourself a copy is a good way to keep the
information safe and accessible. Make sure
you are fully insured if hiring a car or if you're
taking your own vehicle.

Internet
Many museums, libraries, hotels, restaurants
and cafès offer free Wi-Fi. Just remember
these are not secure connections so it is not
advisable to use them for online banking or
other financial transactions.

Money → *For up-to-date exchange rates,*
see www.xe.com.
The British currency is the pound sterling
(£), divided into 100 pence (p). Coins come
in denominations of 1p, 2p, 5p, 10p, 20p,
50p, £1 and £2. Bank of England banknotes
are legal tender in Scotland, in addition to
those issued by the Bank of Scotland, Royal
Bank of Scotland and Clydesdale Bank.
These Scottish banknotes (bills) come in
denominations of £5, £10, £20, £50 and
£100 and regardless of what you are told
by shopkeepers in England the notes are
legal tender in the rest of Britain.

Banks
The larger towns and villages have a branch
of at least one of the big 4 high street
banks – **Bank of Scotland**, **Royal Bank
of Scotland**, **Clydesdale** and **Lloyds TSB
Scotland**. Bank opening hours are Mon-Fri
from 0930 to between 1600 and 1700. Some
larger branches may also be open later
on Thu and on Sat mornings. In small and
remote places, and on some islands, there
may be only a mobile bank which runs to a
set timetable. This timetable will be available
from the local post office. See also page 85.

Banks are usually the best places to
change money and cheques. You can
withdraw cash from selected banks and
ATMs (or cashpoints as they are called in
Britain) with your cash and credit card.
Though using a debit or credit card is by

far the easiest way of keeping in funds, you must check with your bank what the total charges will be; this can be as high as 4-5% in some cases. In more remote parts, and especially on the islands, ATMs are few and far between and it is important to keep a ready supply of cash on you at all times and many guesthouses in the remoter reaches of Scotland will still request payment in cash. Outside the ferry ports on most of the smaller islands, you won't find an ATM. Your bank will give you a list of locations where you can use your card. Bank of Scotland and Royal Bank take Lloyds and Barclays cash cards; Clydesdale takes HSBC and National Westminster cards. Bank of Scotland, Clydesdale and most building society cashpoints are part of the Link network and accept all affiliated cards. See also Credit cards below. In addition to ATMs, bureaux de change can be used outside banking hours. These can be found in most city centres and also at the main airports and train stations. Note that some charge high commissions for changing cheques. Those at international airports, however, often charge less than banks and will change pound sterling cheques for free. Avoid changing money or cheques in hotels, as the rates are usually very poor.

Credit cards
Most hotels, shops and restaurants accept the major credit cards such as MasterCard and Visa and, less frequently, Amex, though some places may charge for using them. They may be less useful in more remote rural areas and smaller establishments such as B&Bs, which will often only accept cash or cheques.

Visa and Mastercard holders can use most ATMs; Amex card holders the Link network.

Currency cards
If you don't want to carry lots of cash, prepaid currency cards allow you to preload money from your bank account, fixed at the day's exchange rate. They look like a credit or debit card and are issued by specialist money changing companies, such as Travelex and Caxton FX. You can top up and check your balance by phone, online and sometimes by text.

Money transfers
If you need money urgently, the quickest way to have it sent to you is to have it wired to the nearest bank via Western Union, www.westernunion.co.uk, or Money-gram, www.moneygram.com. Charges are on a sliding scale; ie it will cost proportionately less to wire out more money. Money can also be wired by Thomas Cook, www.thomasexchangeglobal.co.uk, or transferred via a bank draft, but this can take up to a week.

Opening hours
Businesses are usually open Mon-Sat 0900-1800. In Glasgow and many town cities, many shops open later (and later still on a Thu usually till 2000). Many open on a Sun but with shorter hours – so they will open later and close earlier – generally 1200-1700.

Post
Most post offices are open Mon-Fri 0900 to 1730 and Sat 0900-1230 or 1300. Smaller sub-post offices are closed for an hour at lunch (1300-1400) and many of them operate out of a shop. Post offices keep the same half-day closing times as shops.

Stamps can be bought at post offices, but also from vending machines outside, and also at many newsagents. A 1st-class letter weighing up to 100 g to anywhere in the UK cost 60p or 90p (Large Letter) and should arrive the following day, while 2nd-class letters weighing up to 100 g cost 50p or 69p (Large Letter) take between 2-4 days. For more information about Royal Mail postal services, call T08457-740740, or visit www.royalmail.com.

Safety
Like any large city Glasgow has safe and less safe areas. Commonsense as always applies:

don't carry valuables around and flaunting wealth and expensive camera kit, phones etc is definitely not a good idea. Glasgow's rowdy drinking culture can make walking around at weekends, on match days and during the evening especially unnerving. Although Glasgow is notorious for violent crime most incidents are confined to a small minority of the natives and their obsessions: so stick clear of alcohol, drugs, gang and football rivalry.

Telephone → Country code +44.
Useful numbers: operator T100; international operator T155; directory enquiries T192; overseas directory enquiries T153.

Most public payphones are operated by **British Telecom** (BT) and can be found in towns and cities, though less so in rural areas. Numbers of public phone booths have declined in recent years due to the advent of the mobile phone, so don't rely on being able to find a payphone wherever you go. BT payphones take either coins (20p, 50p and £1) or chargecards, which are available at newsagents and post offices displaying the BT logo. Some payphones also accept credit cards.

For most countries (including Europe, USA and Canada) calls are cheapest Mon-Fri between 1800 and 0800 and all day Sat-Sun. For Australia and New Zealand it's cheapest to call from 1430-1930 and from 2400-0700 every day. Area codes are not needed if calling from within the same area. Any number prefixed by 0800 or 0500 is free to the caller; 08457 numbers are charged at local rates and 08705 numbers at the national rate. To call Scotland from overseas, dial 011 from USA and Canada, 0011 from Australia and 00 from New Zealand, followed by 44, then the area code, minus the 1st zero, then the number. To call overseas from Scotland dial 00 followed by the country code. Country codes include: Australia 61; Ireland 353; New Zealand 64; South Africa 27; USA and Canada 1.

Smoking
Smoking is banned in all enclosed and semi-enclosed public spaces.

Time
Greenwich Mean Time (GMT) is used from late-Oct to late-Mar, after which time the clocks go forward 1 hr to British Summer Time (BST). GMT is 5 hrs ahead of US Eastern Standard Time and 10 hrs behind Australian Eastern Standard Time.

Tipping
Believe it or not, people in Scotland do leave tips. In a restaurant you should leave a tip of 10-15% if you are satisfied with the service. If the bill already includes a service charge, you needn't add a further tip. Tipping is not normal in pubs or bars. Taxi drivers will expect a tip for longer journeys, usually of around 10%; and most hairdressers will also expect a tip. As in most other countries, porters, bellboys and waiters in more upmarket hotels rely on tips to supplement their meagre wages.

Tourist information
Glasgow and the Clyde Valley's main tourist information office is currently at 170 Buchanan St, T0141-204 4400, visitscotland.com/glasgow.

Tourist offices – called tourist information centres (TICs) – can be found in most Scottish towns. Their addresses, phone numbers and opening hours are listed in the relevant sections of this book. Opening hours vary depending on the time of year, and many of the smaller offices are closed during the winter months. All tourist offices provide information on accommodation, public transport, local attractions and restaurants, as well as selling books, local guides, maps and souvenirs. Many also have free street plans and leaflets describing local walks. They can also book accommodation for you, for a small fee.

Museums, galleries and historic houses

Most of Scotland's tourist attractions, apart from the large museums and art galleries in the main cities, are open only from Easter-Oct. Full details of opening hours and admission charges are given in the relevant sections of this guide.

Over 100 of the country's most prestigious sights, and 75,000 ha of beautiful countryside, are cared for by the **National Trust for Scotland (NTS)**, Hermiston Quay, 5 Cultins Rd, Edinburgh EH11 4DF, T0844-493 2100, T0131-458 0303, www.nts.org.uk. National Trust properties are indicated in this guide as 'NTS', and entry charges and opening hours are given for each property.

Historic Scotland (HS), Longmore House, Salisbury Pl, Edinburgh EH9 1SH, T0131-668 8600, www.historic-scotland.gov.uk, manages more than 330 of Scotland's most important castles, monuments and other historic sites. Historic Scotland properties are indicated as 'HS', and admission charges and opening hours are also given in this guide. Historic Scotland offers an Explorer Pass, which allows free entry to 78 of its properties including Glasgow Cathedral and Bothwell Castle plus Edinburgh and Stirling castles. A 3-day pass (can be used over 5 consecutive days) costs £29, children £17, concessions £24, family £58, 7-day pass (valid for 14 days) £38, £22, £31, £76.

Many other historic buildings are owned by local authorities, and admission is cheap, or in many cases free. Most fee-paying attractions give a discount or concession for senior citizens, the unemployed, full-time students and children under 16 (those under 5 are admitted free everywhere). Proof of age or status must be shown. Many of Scotland's stately homes are still owned and occupied by the landed gentry, and admission is usually between £5 and £10.

Finding out more

The best way of finding out more information for your trip to Scotland is to contact **Visit Scotland** (aka the Scottish Tourist Board), or www.visitbritain.com. Both organizations can provide a wealth of free literature and information such as maps, city guides and accommodation brochures. If particularly interested in ensuring your visit coincides with a major festival or sporting event, it's also worthwhile having a look at **EventScotland**'s website, www.eventscotland.org. Travellers with special needs should also contact **VisitScotland** or their nearest **VisitBritain** office. If you want more detailed information on a particular area, contact the specific tourist boards.

Visas and immigration

Visa regulations are subject to change, so it is essential to check with your local British embassy, high commission or consulate before leaving home. Citizens of all European countries – except Albania, Bosnia Herzegovina, Kosovo, Macedonia, Moldova, Turkey, Serbia and all former Soviet republics (other than the Baltic states) – require only a passport to enter Britain and can generally stay for up to 3 months. Citizens of Australia, Canada, New Zealand, South Africa or the USA can stay for up to 6 months, providing they have a return ticket and sufficient funds to cover their stay. Citizens of most other countries require a visa from the commission or consular office in the country of application.

The **Foreign and Commonwealth Office (FCO)**, T0207-270 1500, www.fco.gov.uk, has an excellent website, which provides details of British immigration and visa requirements. Also the **Home Office UK Border Agency** is responsible for UK immigration matters and its website is a good place to start for anyone hoping visit, work, study or emigrate to the UK. Call the immigration enquiry bureau on T0870-6067 766 or visit www.bia.homeoffice.gov.uk.

For visa extensions also contact the Home Office UK Border Agency via the above number or its website. The agency can also be reached at Lunar House,

Wellesley Rd, Croydon, London CR9. Citizens of Australia, Canada, New Zealand, South Africa or the USA wishing to stay longer than 6 months will need an Entry Clearance Certificate from the British High Commission in their country. For more details, contact your nearest British embassy, consulate or high commission, or the Foreign and Commonwealth Office in London.

Weights and measures

Imperial and metric systems are both in use. Distances on roads are measured in miles and yards, drinks poured in pints and gills, but generally, the metric system is used elsewhere.

Volunteering

Contact **VDS** on T01786-479593 or consult www.volunteerscotland.org.uk.

British Trust for Conservation Volunteers, Sedum House, Mallard Way, Doncaster DN4 8DB, T01302-388 883, www.btcv.org. Get fit in the 'green gym', planting hedges, creating wildlife gardens or improving footpaths. **Earthwatch**, 256 Banbury Rd, Oxford OX2 7DE, T01865-318838. Team up with scientists studying our furry friends. **Jubilee Sailing Trust**, Hazel Rd, Southampton, T023-804 9108, www.jst. org. uk. Work on deck on an adventure holiday. **National Trust for Scotland**, Hermiston Quay, 5 Cultins Rd, Edinburgh EH11 4DF, T0844-493 2100/0131-458 0303, www. nts.org.uk. Among a number of Scotland based charities that offer volunteering opportunities. You could find yourself helping restore buildings on St Kilda or taking part in an archaeological dig on Loch Lomondside.

Contents

Footprint features

Glasgow

Glasgow

Those who have come to see the sights won't be disappointed, for there are some world-class museums and galleries, many of which are free. The city's most popular attraction is the Burrell Collection, a state-of-the-art building stuffed with priceless antiquities from around the world. In the West End is the Kelvingrove Art Gallery and Museum while further south is the Riverside Museum. Across town in the East End is the fascinating People's Palace, which tells the story of this great city, while on the north side of the city centre is the strangely beguiling Tenement House, a time capsule of life in pre-war Glasgow. And then there's Charles Rennie Mackintosh, Glasgow's answer to Gaudí. His masterpiece, the Glasgow School of Art, is not to be missed.

Glasgow city centre covers the large area from Charing Cross train station and the M8 in the west to Glasgow Green in the east, near the cathedral. The heart of the city is George Square and to the east is the renovated Merchant City, which together with the streets west of George Square, forms the commercial and business centre. Here the Palladian mansions of the Tobacco Lords have been reclaimed by the professional classes as a fashionable place to eat, drink and play. The main shopping streets in the centre are Sauchiehall Street, Buchanan Street and Argyle Street.

Further east, in stark contrast, is the East End, a traditional working-class stronghold, and to the north is the oldest part of Glasgow, around the medieval cathedral.

The West End begins across the ugly scar of the M8. This is the home of the University and is the city's main student quarter, with many of its best bars, cafés and restaurants. An area of grand Victorian townhouses and sweeping terraces it is also home of some of the city's best museums. South of the Clyde are the more sedate suburbs of the South Side. To the southwest, in Pollok Country Park, are two of Glasgow's main attractions, Pollok House and the Burrell Collection.

24 hours in the city

Twenty-four hours in Glasgow is just not enough, but if you're really pushed for time the following suggested itinerary will give a brief indication of why this is now considered one of the most exciting cities in Europe.

Start the day at the **People's Palace** on Glasgow Green for an introduction to the city's history. Head across to **Sauchiehall Street** for mid-morning coffee in the **Willow Tea Rooms** and admire the elegant interior design of Charles Rennie Mackintosh. Down to **Princes Square** for a spot of shopping, followed by a walk around the **Merchant City** and lunch in **Babbity Bowster**.

After lunch, head up to the **School of Art**, take a tour and find out what all the fuss is about. Then head across the M8 to St George's Cross Underground and take the subway to Hillhead for a browse round the trendy shops of **Byres Road**. Stop for an aperitif in one of the many cool bars and cafés then it's off to dinner to the one-and-only **Ubiquitous Chip**. Take a cab back to the city centre for a cruise round some of the hip pre-club bars before hitting one of the city's legendary clubs for a good old boogie.

Arriving in Glasgow

Tourist information

Glasgow and the Clyde Valley's main **tourist information office** ① *170 Buchanan St, T0141-204 4400, www.seeglasgow.com*, provides an excellent service with a wide selection of maps and leaflets and a free accommodation booking service. You can also buy travel passes, theatre tickets, arrange car rental and exchange currency at their bureau de change.

For travel information head to the **Strathclyde Travel Centres** ① *T0141-332 6811, at Buchanan St Bus station Mon-Sat 0630-2230, Sun 0700-2230 (last ticket sales 2130) or St Enoch Subway station Mon-Tue 0830-1730, Wed 0900-1700, Thu-Sat 0830-1730, Sun 1000-1700*. They can provide maps, leaflets and timetables. Travel information is also available from **Traveline Scotland** ① *T0871-200 2233, www.travelinescotland.com*.

Background

Glasgow was founded in 543 AD when St Mungo built a church in what was then called Glas-ghu (meaning 'dear green place'). The establishment of a cathedral in the 12th century and Scotland's second university in the 15th century brought status to the city and it was made a royal burgh in 1454.

But Glasgow played little part in the political or economic history of medieval Scotland. It was largely ignored during the bitter wars with England and most of the country's trade was with the Low Countries via the east coast ports.

The city's commercial prosperity came in the 17th century, when it began importing tobacco, sugar, cotton and other goods from the Americas. It began to expand westwards from the medieval centre of the High Street (with the exception of the cathedral, nothing of medieval Glasgow remains). Glasgow's location in the Clyde valley, surrounded by developing coalfields and with deep-water docks only 20 miles from the sea, ensured its development during the Industrial Revolution, in the late 18th century. The city grew rapidly with an influx of immigrants, mainly from the West Highlands, to work in the cotton mills. The deepening of the Clyde up to the Broomielaw, near the heart of the city, and the coming of the railway in the 19th century made the city one of the great industrial centres of the world.

It continued to expand rapidly between the late 18th and early 19th centuries, growing five-fold in only 50 years, and was further swelled by thousands of Irish immigrants fleeing Ireland to escape famine and to seek work. By the mid-19th century Glasgow's population had reached 400,000 and it could justifiably call itself the 'second city of the empire'. The Victorians built most of the city's most notable buildings, along with the acres of congested tenements that would later become notorious slums.

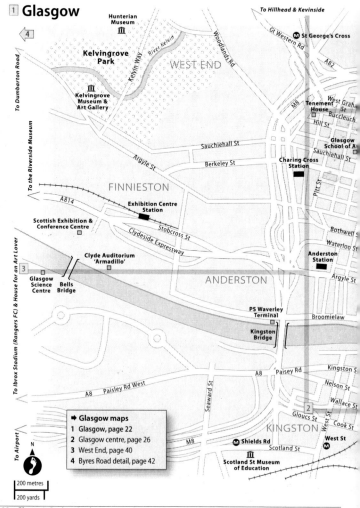

Glasgow

➡ **Glasgow maps**
1 Glasgow, page 22
2 Glasgow centre, page 26
3 West End, page 40
4 Byres Road detail, page 42

Since the Second World War and the decline of shipbuilding and heavy industries, Glasgow's population has fallen from over a million to less than 700,000: the result of planning policies designed to decant its population from slum tenements into new towns such as East Kilbride and Combernauld outside the city. During the recession of the late 1970s, Glasgow suffered more than most but instead of confronting central government, Glasgow embarked on a bold plan to reinvent itself and shake off the shackles of its industrial past. With its customary energy and wit, the city launched the 'Glasgow's Miles Better' promotional campaign in 1983 which led to the 1988 Garden Festival, 1990's year as European City of Culture and City of

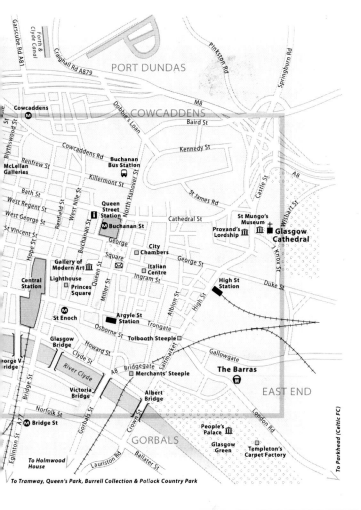

Architecture and Design in 1999. In 2014 it hosts the Commonwealth Games and in 2015 the Turner Prize for contemporary art lands at the Tramway arts hub, in the city that has provided so many of its recent winners. The Merchant City's abandoned warehouses of the recession have been transformed and filled by creative businesses and apartments, and down by the Clyde impressive contemporary architecture housing media hubs, venues and museums has brought work and play back to the river. While some areas and communities have been reinvigorated others still suffer abject poverty and social problems. Glasgow may still suffer urban deprivation, but it has regained its old confidence and transformed itself into a post-industrial city with manifold attractions and a thriving cultural scene.

City centre to the East End → *For listings, see pages 59-85.*

Many of the city's most important buildings and institutions can be found between North Street (the M8) in the west and Gallowgate in the east, and from Cowcaddens in the north down to the Clyde. A few examples of medieval architecture remains: most notably heading east at the Cathedral and the mercantile monuments around Mercat Cross. Centering on St Vincent Street and George Square is a grid of streets lined with grandiose Victorian and turn-of-the-20th-century architecture, reflecting Glasgow's power as part of the British Empire. Towards the Clyde are the mansions of the Tobacco Lords – once abandoned and now transformed into the buzzing Merchant City, full of smart shops, bars and restaurants. From Trongate to the Clyde and east to Glasgow Green and the Barras, the territory gets scruffier and looser with new developments arising from the old industries. It's an interesting mix of traditional working class streets with newer artsy businesses and galleries.

George Square
The heart of modern Glasgow is George Square, which makes the obvious starting point for a tour of the city centre, as the tourist information centre is located here, on the south side; see page 21. Amongst the many statues which adorn the square are those of Queen Victoria, Prince Albert, Sir Walter Scott, Robert Burns, Sir Robert Peel and James Watt. The square was named after George III and laid out in 1781. However for several years it was not much more than a watery patch of ground where horses were taken to be slaughtered and puppies to be drowned. The plan was to make it an upmarket, elegant square with private gardens at its centre. However many of the buildings – designed by the Adam brothers – were never built, while the gardens didn't last long as Glaswegians objected to such an obvious display of privilege and ripped the railings down in disgust. The square only became the heart of the city when the council decided to make it the location for the **City Chambers** ① *T0141-287 2000, free guided tours, Mon-Fri at 1030 and 1430*, the most visible symbol of Glasgow's position as Second City of the Empire. Among the other fine Victorian buildings on the square the grandiose chambers fill the east side and are a wonderful testament to the optimism and aspiration of Victorian Glasgow. The building was designed in Italian Renaissance style by William Young and the interior is even more impressive than its façade. The imposing arcaded marble entrance hall is decorated with elaborate mosaics (over half a million Venetian tiles). Linger a while with the ubiquitous school groups to listen to the banter and verse for memorizing the four emblems of the St Mungo's coat of arms that recall legends: Here's the Bird that never flew, Here's the Tree that never grew, Here's the Bell that never rang, Here's the Fish that never swam. A Carrara marble staircase leads up to a great banqueting hall with a wonderful arched ceiling, leaded glass windows and paintings depicting scenes from the city's history.

Architecture

Glasgow has a wealth of impressive architecture in grandiose sandstone and contemporary steel and glass. Sandstone predominates from the medieval remnants around the Cathedral, 17th-century mercantile structures of Trongate and the hulking palaces, mansions and tobacco warehouses of Victorian Glasgow's Imperial heyday. As well as the celebrated buildings of Alexander 'Greek' Thomson and William Young's City Chambers there are mighty totems to industry, banking and civic life all over the city centre and Merchant City, especially along St Vincent, Ingram and Glassford streets. Many of the Merchant City's once abandoned old warehouses and public buildings have been re-purposed making the area a smart and buzzing district. The West End has the splendour of Kelvingrove, Italianate Park Circus and cobbled lanes that recall a pastoral past.

Despite the 1960s planners demolishing old tenements and strangling the city with a motorway there have been some attempts at regeneration of late. Attempts are being made to reconnect the city, its people and the river Clyde. Along the Clyde is a new crop of bridges and bold architecture: Atlantic Quay and 'squiggly' bridge, the Clyde Auditorium (dubbed the Armadillo), Glasgow Science Centre, BBC HQ Pacific Quay and Zaha Hadid's Riverside Museum. See also page 88.

On the northwest corner of George Square, opposite Queen Street Station, is **Merchants House** ① *7 West George St, T0141-221 8272, www.merchantshouse.org.uk*, a fine Victorian building topped with a golden ship that houses the Glasgow Chamber of Commerce and hosts lunchtime classical music concerts. The Merchants House bought part of the Wester Craigs estate in 1650 and funded the city's Necropolis in the 1830s (see page 32). An architectural competition was begun in 2012 to revamp George Square's gardens.

Gallery of Modern Art (GoMA)

① *Royal Exchange Sq, T0141-287 3050, www.glasgowlife.org.uk, Mon-Wed and Sat 1000-1700, Thu 1000-2000, Fri and Sun 1100-1700, free.*
Look out for the equestrian statue of the Duke of Wellington, now traditionally crowned with a traffic cone, at Royal Exchange Square. The stately building here with Corinthian columns houses the Gallery of Modern Art (GoMA). It dates from 1778, when it was built upon a muddy Cow Lane as the Cunninghame Mansion, home to one of Glasgow's wealthy Tobacco Lords. It became a branch of the Royal Bank of Scotland in 1817 and 10 years later the magnificent portico was added to the front and the building then became the Royal Exchange, the city's main business centre. It then housed a library, until its reopening in 1996 as one of the city's newest, and its most controversial, art venues, drawing the ire of many a critic for its unashamed eclecticism and populism. The gallery features contemporary works from artists worldwide in four galleries, plus a great basement café. The cavernous main space on the ground floor with classical features usually features bold works by big names such as Jim Lambie, Bridget Riley and David Mach. Upper galleries have more natural light and focus on group shows that often tackle challenging themes. An exhibit in the shOUT show (2009) – Made in God's Image – in which visitors were invited to add comments to the pages of a bible, attracted much debate and 600 complaints.

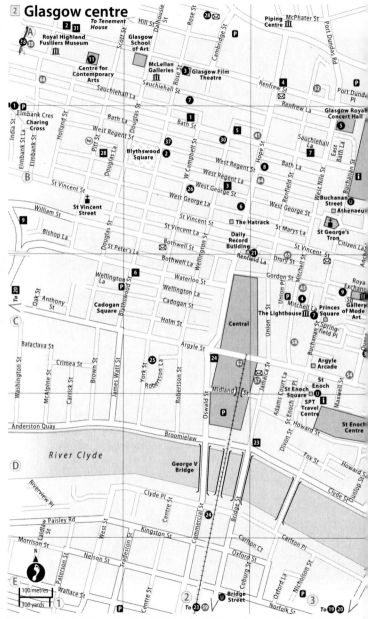

Glasgow centre

To Tenement House
Royal Highland Fusiliers Museum
Centre for Contemporary Arts
Glasgow School of Art
McLellan Galleries
Glasgow Film Theatre
Piping Centre
Glasgow Royal Concert Hall
Charing Cross
Elmbank Cres
Blythswood Square
St Vincent Street
Buchanan Street
St George's Tron
Athenaeum
The Hatrack
Daily Record Building
Cadogan Square
The Lighthouse
Central
Princes Square
Gallery of Modern Art
St Vincent Street
Royal Exchange
Argyle Arcade
St Enoch Square
SPT Travel Centre
St Enoch Centre
River Clyde
George V Bridge
Bridge Street

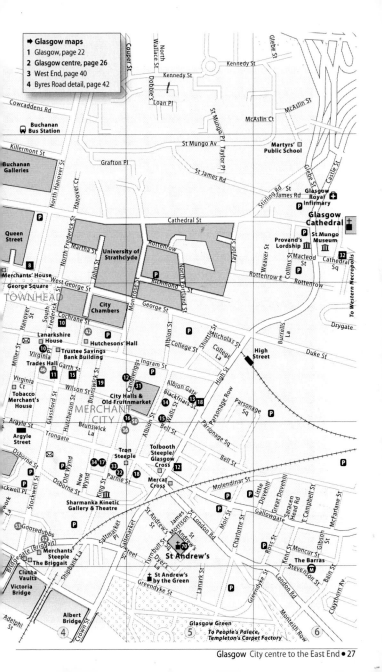

➜ **Glasgow maps**
1 Glasgow, page 22
2 Glasgow centre, page 26
3 West End, page 40
4 Byres Road detail, page 42

Couper St
North Wallace St
Dobbie's
Kennedy St
Loan Pl
North Wallace St
Gleba St
Kennedy St
McAslin St
McAslin Ct

Cowcaddens Rd
St Mungo Pl Taylor Pl
St Mungo Av
St James Rd
Stirling Rd
James Rd
Castle St
Glebe St

🚌 **Buchanan Bus Station**
Killermont St
Grafton Pl
St James Rd
Martyrs' Public School
Glasgow Royal Infirmary ✚

Buchanan Galleries
Cathedral St
Glasgow Cathedral ✚

P
Queen Street
West George St
North Hanover St
Martha St
John St
University of Strathclyde
Rottenrow
Taylor St
Weaver St
Provand's Lordship 🏛
St Mungo Museum 🏛
Macleod St
Cathedral St
32
Cathedral Sq

8
Merchants' House
George Square
TOWNHEAD
West George St
George St
Richmond
North Portland St
Collins St
Rottenrow E
Rottenrow
To Western Necropolis
Drygate

P
Hanover St
South Frederick St
Cochrane St
10
City Chambers
42
Lanarkshire House
Hutchesons' Hall
Albion St
Nicholas St
College St
College La
Shuttle St
High Street
Burrells La
Duke St

🖂 **10**
Trustee Savings Bank Building
Trades Hall **11** **36**
Virginia St
Garth St
15
Ingram St
Candleriggs
12
Albion Gate
Blackfriars St
High St
Parsonage Row
High Street

Virginia Ct
Wilson St
Brunswick St
31
City Halls & Old Fruitmarket
14
13 **18**
Parsonage Sq
P

Tobacco Merchant's House
MERCHANT CITY
Brunswick La
Albion St
16 **50**
Bell St
Watt St
15
Parsonage Sq

■ **Argyle Street**
Glassford St
Hutcheson St
36
Trongate
Argyle St
Bell St
P

Osborne St
Old Wynd
34 **17**
Tron Steeple
22
18
Tolbooth Steeple/ Glasgow Cross
12
Molendinar St

🖂
New Wynd
Parnie St
Mercat Cross
Little Dovenhill
Great Dovenhill
Gallowgate
Saraten Head Rd
E Campbell St
McFarlane St

ckwell St
Osborne St
King St
Sharmanka Kinetic Gallery & Theatre
St Andrew's St
James St
London Rd
Moir St
Charlotte St
Ross St
Kent St
Moncur St
The Barras
Gibson St
Stevenson St
Bain St
Claythorn Av
Monteith Row

53
Goosedubbs
Saltmarket
St Andrew's St
Turnbull St
St Andrew's
70
St Andrew's St
Greendyke St
London Rd
Kent St
🅜
Claythorn Av

Merchants Steeple
The Briggait
Bridgegate (Briggait)
Shipbank La
Steel St
Saltmarket
✚ **St Andrew's by the Green**
Greendyke St
Lanark St
Gt Dovenhill
London Rd
Stevenson St

Clutha Vaults
Victoria Bridge
Adelphi St
Albert Bridge
Crown St
Glasgow Green
To People's Palace, Templeton's Carpet Factory

4 **5** **6**

Merchant City

The grid-plan of streets to the east of George Square as far as the High Street form the Merchant City, where the Tobacco Lords built their magnificent Palladian mansions. They made Glasgow the most important tobacco-trading city in Europe and can also take the credit for it being one of the lung cancer capitals of the world by the mid-20th century. The street names here reflect the traders and sources of the Tobacco Lords' wealth.

This part of the city was once a bustling trade centre and money has been poured into the restoration of its 18th-century warehouses and homes in an attempt to revitalize and regenerate the city's old historic core. Though many of the buildings are little more than façades, the investment has succeeded in attracting expensive designer clothes shops and a plethora of stylish bistros, cafés and bars, which are packed with the city's young professionals and media types. It's a vibrant area full of handsome architecture, independent bars and boutique shopping.

Trades Hall ⓘ *85 Glassford St, T0141-552 2418, www.tradeshallglasgow.co.uk, free entry subject to availability: Mon-Fri 0900-1600, Sat 0900-1200, guided tours Tue 1000 by appointment only*, is Glasgow's oldest secular building. It was designed by Robert Adam and built in 1794 as the headquarters of the city's 14 trade guilds and still serves its original purpose. The Grand Hall is an impressive sight, lined with a Belgian silk tapestry depicting the work of a range of former city trades such as bonnetmakers (not much call for them nowadays) and cordiners (bootmakers).

St John Street south of the City Chambers is the pedestrianized concourse of the **Italian Centre** with its continental air of white-aproned waiters dashing between smart cafés and boutiques. Four classical sculptures – *Italia*, *Mercury*, *Mercurial*, and *Mercurius* – by Alexander Stoddart contrast with the centre's designer label fetishism. Seek out the centre's courtyard calm of Shona Kinloch's enigmatic *Thinking of Bella* (1994) figures spanning a minimalist water feature.

Glasgow centre map key

Where to stay 🛏
Adelaide's 1 *B2*
Babbity Bowster 18 *C5*
Baby Abode 5 *B2*
Brunswick 19 *C4*
Carlton George 3 *B2*
Cathedral House 32 *B6*
CitizenM 4 *A3*
Crowne Plaza 20 *C1*
Euro Hostel 23 *D3*
Hilton 9 *B1*
Indigo 6 *C2*
Malmaison 28 *B1*
Max Serviced
  Apartments 7 *B3*
Millennium 8 *B4*
Rab Ha's 15 *C4*
Radisson SAS 24 *C2*
Rennie Mackintosh
  Art School 2 *A1*
The Serviced Apartment
  Company 10 *C4*

The Spires 11 *C4*
Tolbooth Apartments 12 *D5*
Victorian House 31 *A1*

Restaurants 🍴
Amber Regent 8 *B3*
Arta 15 *C5*
Ashoka Southside 19 *E3*
Baby Grand 1 *A1*
Brian Maule at Chardon
  d'Or 2 *B2*
Buongiorno 23 *E2*
Café Cosmo 3 *A2*
Café Cossachok 17 *D4*
Café Gandolfi 14 *C5*
Café Source 70 *D5*
City Merchant 12 *C5*
The Corinthian Club 10 *C4*
Dhabba 16 *C5*
Doocot Café & Bar 4 *C3*
Esca 18 *D5*
Fratelli Sarti 30 *B2*

Gamba 26 *B2*
Glasgow Noodle Bar 38 *A1*
Greek Golden
  Kebab 20 *E3*
The Green Room 5 *B3*
Ho Wong 25 *C2*
Ichiban Japanese
  Noodle Café 35 *C3*
Metropolitan 31 *C5*
Mono 34 *D4*
Mussel Inn 6 *B2*
Rogano's 9 *C3*
Saramago Café Bar 11 *A1*
Schottische 13 *C5*
Spice Garden 24 *D2*
Stereo 21 *C3*
Trattoria Gia 33 *D4*
Tron Theatre 22 *D4*
Wee Curry Shop 28 *A2*
Where the Monkey
  Sleeps 37 *B2*
Willow Tea Rooms 7 *A2, C3*

Bars & clubs 🍸
Archaos 54 *C3*
Arches 62 *C2*
Bar Ten 58 *C3*
Blackfriars 50 *C5*
Bloc 41 *B3*
Delmonica's 46 *C4*
Flying Duck 32 *A3*
Garage 39 *A1*
Griffin 68 *A1*
Horse Shoe 65 *C3*
Merchant Pride 36 *D4*
Pot Still 64 *B3*
Samuel Dow's 59 *E2*
Scotia 53 *D4*
Sub Club 57 *C3*
Tunnel 43 *C3*
Underground 42 *C4*
Victoria 52 *D4*

The Merchant City has fine architecture and many of its abandoned warehouses have been transformed into chic venues. At 158 Ingram Street is **Hutchesons' Hall**, a distinguished blond ashlar Georgian building – with a gleaming white paint-job. It was built in 1802 by David Hamilton, in neoclassical style with a traditional Scottish 'townhouse' steeple. It was once home of the Scottish Educational Trust, a charitable institution founded by the 17th-century lawyer brothers George and Thomas Hutcheson, which provided almshouses and schools for the city. Their statues gaze down towards the site of the original almshouse in Trongate. Going east at 98 Ingram Street is **Ramshorn Kirk** (1824), a Gothic Revival-style church with 37-m-high clocktower. Strathclyde University's theatre and music groups now use the space. Along nearby Albion Street and Candleriggs there's a cluster of excellent eateries including **Café Gandolfi** (see page 65) and performance venues, such as **City Halls** and **Old Fruitmarket** (see page 76). On Brunswick Street there's the former **Glasgow Sheriff Court**, a sandstone Victorian building with Ionic columns. Its interiors were masterfully re-designed to house the Scottish Youth Theatre in 2005.

At the corner of Ingram Street and Glassford Street is the lavish **Trustee Savings Bank** building, designed by that prodigious talent, JJ Burnet, in 1900. Nearby, on Ingram Street, is another fine building – **Lanarkshire House** – designed by his father, John Burnet, along with two more of Glasgow's greatest architects, David Hamilton and James Salmon Junior. It dates from 1879 and has now been opened as the **Corinthian** (see page 65), a combination of bars, restaurants, a casino and meeting rooms.

At 42 Miller Street is the restored **Tobacco Merchant's House**, the Merchant City's oldest surviving house, built by John Craig in 1775 as one of a row of villas. In 1782 it was purchased by Robert Findlay of Easterhill, a tobacco importer. It is now the home of the **Scottish Civic Trust** ① *T0141-221 1466*, which runs Doors Open Days (www.doorsopendays.org.uk) that allow occasional public access to this building and similar architectural treasures. Findlay's son, also called Robert, developed the nearby Virginia Street and Buildings (1814-1817). The Tobacco Exchange and warehouses were replaced by a swanky leisure, shopping and housing development called Virginia Court in 2010.

Trongate, Glasgow Cross and around

The Merchant City is bounded to the east by the High Street and to the south by Trongate (the 'tron' is the weighing machine introduced in 1491 to weigh and tax goods entering the city). These two streets meet at **Glasgow Cross**, once the centre of trade and administration and regarded as the city centre until the coming of the railway in the mid-19th century. In the centre of the intersection stands the 38-m-high **Tolbooth Steeple**, one of only three crowned steeples in the country. This is the only remnant of the original tolbooth built in 1626, which housed the courthouse and prison (described by Sir Walter Scott in *Rob Roy*). The original edifice had unedifying spikes on the walls for the decapitated heads of felons. The **Mercat Cross**, next to the steeple, is a 1929 replica of the medieval original.

The nearby **Tron Steeple** is the only surviving part of St Mary's Church, built in 1637. This church was accidentally burned down by drunken members of the aptly named Glasgow Hellfire Club in 1793. After a meeting, they went to the church to warm themselves by a fire, which they built up until it got out of control. The steeple has been incorporated into the modern frontage of the **Tron Theatre** (see page 78) and the interior of the replacement church forms the theatre auditorium. After the transformation of the Merchant City, the City Council aims to make art-led regeneration continue south towards the Clyde. The multi-faceted arts centre **Trongate 103** (see below) and the **WASPS artist studios** ① *141 Bridgegate, www.waspsstudios.org.uk*, housed in the handsome old fish market known as The Briggait, and **South Block** on King Street are its starting point. Trongate and WASPS stage exhibitions. Head towards the three-tiered 50-m-high **Merchants' Steeple** (1665) at Bridgegate to see the remnants of the original Merchants' House (1651-1659) or Guildhall, which is now part of The Briggait. Between The Briggait and Trongate, around King Street, is a lively area crammed with contemporary art galleries and studios, and laid-back arty venues, bars, and cafés. It's a good hunting ground for original gifts and inspiration.

Don't miss **Trongate 103** ⓘ *T0141-276 8380, www.trongate103.com, Tue-Sat 1000-1700, Sun 1200-1700, free*, an impressive arts centre which opened in 2009, housed in a hulking Edwardian warehouse where international artists and the public mingle. It's a wonderful place to see and purchase contemporary art. A cavernous contemporary atrium leads to five floors of studios and galleries. The interesting residents include Glasgow Print Studio, Street Level Photoworks, Transmission Gallery, GMAC Film Studios, Glasgow Project Room, Project Ability and Sharmanka. The darkly magic junk-world of the **Sharmanka Kinetic Theatre** ⓘ *T0141-552 7080, www.sharmanka.com, £4-8, daily 45-min shows Wed-Sun 1500 and 70-min shows Thu and Sun 2000*, will appeal to kids and adults alike. The Sharmanka's (from the Russian for hurdy gurdy) fantastical mechanical inventions are the work of Edward Bersudsky and Tatyana Jakovskaya, whose kinetic sculptures of carved wood and scrap are set amid atmospheric lighting and haunting Eastern European music. Check the website for latest events and live music programme. On Trongate 103's ground floor **Café Cossachock** (see page 65) serves food and refreshments and stages jazz and world music events.

East End → *For listings, see pages 59-85.*

East of Glasgow Cross, Gallowgate and London Road lead into the city's East End, only a stone's throw from the Merchant City. It may look shabby and rundown by comparison but this is where you can sample a slice of pure Glasgow, especially in **The Barras** ⓘ *weekends, 1930-1630, entrance is marked by the red gates on Gallowgate,* a huge market spread out around the streets and alleys south of Gallowgate. You could spend days rummaging around through acres of cheap, new and second-hand goods. A lot of it's junk (dodgy computer games, pirate videos etc) but there are plenty of bargains to be found and there's every chance of unearthing a valuable antique. The real attraction, though, is the distinctive atmosphere of the place and wit and repartee of the market traders.

South of The Barras is the wide expanse of **Glasgow Green**, said to be the oldest public park in Britain. It has been common land since at least medieval times and Glaswegians still have the right to dry their washing here. There are various **monuments** dotted around the park, including a 44-m-high monument to Lord Nelson, erected in 1806, and one to James Watt. The McLennan Arch (1796) was originally part of the Assembly Rooms' façade on Ingram Street. Just to the north of the Green are two of the city's oldest churches, dating from the mid-18th century. In St Andrew's Square is **St Andrew's Church**, one of the finest classical churches in Britain. Sadly neglected for many years, it has now been restored to its Georgian splendour. It no longer functions as a church but has been cleverly converted to house the sleek **Café Source** (see page 67) downstairs and a Scottish music venue upstairs called **St Andrew's in the Square**. You can go upstairs and see the stunning original stained-glass windows and intricate plasterwork. Concerts and ceilidhs are staged throughout the year; tickets are available from the café. Nearby is the episcopal **St Andrew's-by-the-Green**, once known as the Whistlin' Kirk because of the introduction of its organ, a radical move in those days.

On the edge of the green, to the east of the People's Palace, see below, is **Templeton's Carpet Factory**, a bizarre but beautiful structure designed in 1889 by William Leiper in imitation of the Doges' Palace in Venice. Once described as the 'world's finest example of decorative brickwork', it's Britain's best example of polychromatic decoration (in other words, very colourful). The building is now used as a business centre.

People's Palace

ⓘ *T0141-276 0788, www.glasgowlife.org.uk, Tue-Thu and Sat 1000-1700, Fri and Sun 1100-1700, free.*

On the northern end of the green, approached from London Road, is the Victorian red-sandstone People's Palace, opened in 1898 as a folk museum for the East End. The museum gives a real insight into the social and industrial life of this great city from the mid-18th century to the present day. Its galleries display a wealth of artefacts, photographs, cartoons and drawings, and a series of films, music and people's anecdotes. There's a reconstructed 'steamie' (communal laundry) from nearby Ingram Street; brochures extolling the delights of a trip 'Doon the watter' on the Clyde, and video displays on 'the patter' – Glaswegian à la Rab C Nesbitt. The museum doesn't shrink from covering the less salubrious aspects of city history either. There's a display on 'the bevvy' (drink) which includes a barrow once used regularly by the police to wheel drunks home. On the top floor is a powerful ceiling cycle of paintings by Ken Currie marking the Calton Weaver Massacre (1787). In front of the palace is the five-tiered red terracotta Doulton Fountain that commemorated Queen Victoria's Golden Jubilee of 1877. It's the largest terracotta fountain the world: 14 m by

21 m. A visit to the People's Palace should be on everyone's itinerary, particularly if you're interested in scratching beneath the city's surface and getting to know it better. Equally recommended is the adjoining **Winter Gardens and Café** ① *daily 1000-1700*, a huge conservatory housing tropical plants.

Up High Street to the Glasgow Cathedral

Until the 18th century Glasgow consisted only of a narrow ribbon of streets running north from the river past the Glasgow Cross and up the High Street to the cathedral. Then came the city's rapid expansion west and the High Street became a dilapidated backwater. Climbing High Street, you pass under towering old tenements with crow-stepped gables, turrets and balconies and the neglected British Linen Bank. Seek out its crowning statue of Pallas, goddess of wisdom and weaving – plus a plaque to poet Thomas Campbell on the north façade. High Street has an eerie mix of run-down shops approaching the two oldest buildings in the city, Glasgow Cathedral and Provand's Lordship. Opposite Cathedral Square at Rottenrow is red-sandstone **Barony Hall** (1889) with a Gothic spire, now owned by the nearby University.

Glasgow Cathedral

① *Cathedral St, T0141-552 8198, www.glasgowcathedral.com, Apr-Sep Mon-Sat 0930-1730, Sun 1300-1700, Oct-Mar Mon-Sat 0930-1630, Sun 1400-1630, free.*

Glasgow Cathedral is a rather severe-looking early Gothic structure and the only complete medieval cathedral on the Scottish mainland. It was built on the site of St Mungo's original church, established in AD 543, though this has been a place of Christian worship since it was blessed for burial in AD 397 by St Ninian, the earliest missionary recorded in Scottish history. Most of the building was completed in the 13th century though parts were built a century earlier by Bishop Jocelyn. The choir and crypt were added a century later and the building was completed at the end of the 15th century by Robert Blacader, the first Bishop of Glasgow. During the Reformation, the city's last Roman Catholic Archbishop, James Beaton, took off for France with most of the cathedral treasures, just ahead of the townsfolk who proceeded to rid the building of all traces of 'idolatry' by destroying altars, statues, vestments and the valuable library. The present furnishings mostly date from the 19th century and many of the windows have been renewed with modern stained glass. The most outstanding feature in the cathedral is the fan vaulting around St Mungo's tomb in the crypt, one of the very finest examples of medieval architecture in Scotland. There's also fine work in the choir, including a 15th-century stone screen, the only one of its kind left in any pre-Reformation secular (non-monastic) church in Scotland.

Western Necropolis

Behind the cathedral looms a vast burial ground overlooking the city from the top of a high ridge. It was modelled on Père Lachaise cemetery in Paris. Around 3500 tombs have been built here and around 50,000 burials have taken place. Most of the burials took place in the 19th century and the ornate nature of many of the tombs makes it appear as if the city worthies buried here really were trying to take their money with them when they died. It's the ideal vantage point from which to appreciate the cathedral in all its Gothic splendour and many of the tombs are wonderfully ornate. Interred here are the great and the good (and not so good) of Victorian Glasgow – there was no discrimination; anyone could be buried here as long as they could afford it. The graveyard is overseen by a statue of John Knox, the 16th-century firebrand reformer. There's also a monument to William

Miller who penned the nursery rhyme Wee Willie Winkie. Look out for a monument to Chief Constable of the Glasgow Police Alexander McCall. Called the *Celtic Cross* (1888), it's the first solo work by Charles Rennie Mackintosh, whose father William worked as McCall's assistant.

St Mungo Museum of Religious Life and Art

ⓘ *2 Castle St, T0141-276 1625, www.glasgowmuseums.com, Tue-Thu and Sat 1000-1700, Fri and Sun 1100-1700, free.*

In front of the cathedral is the Weetabix-coloured St Mungo Museum, which features a series of displays of arts and artefacts representing the six major world religions, as well as a Japanese Zen garden in the courtyard outside – great for a few moments of quiet contemplation. Highlights include Salvador Dalí's astounding *Christ of St John of the Cross*, purchased by the city from the artist in 1951. You can also see a Native American ceremonial blanket depicting sacred animals, masks used in African initiation rites, and an Islamic prayer rug. Displays on religion in the west of Scotland cover everything from the Temperance movement of the late 19th century, to the religious life of the modern city's vibrant ethnic communities. Don't miss the extremely interesting comments on the visitors' board. There's also a bookshop and café serving hot meals, snacks and drinks.

Provand's Lorship

ⓘ *3 Castle St, T0141-276 1625, www.glasgowmuseums.com, Tue-Thu and Sat 1000-1700, Fri and Sun 1100-1700, free.*

Across the street is the oldest remaining house in Glasgow, built in 1471 as part of a refuge for the city's poor and extended in 1670. It has also served as an inn of rather dubious repute in its time. Now it's a museum devoted mainly to medieval furniture and various domestic items. In the grounds is the tranquil cloistered St. Nicholas Garden with medicinal herbs and intriguing Tontine Heads: stone masks unearthed around the city and collected here. A short walk north from these ancient buildings is **Martyrs' Public School**, Parson Street (off Stirling Road). This school, which was opened in 1897, was one of the first buildings designed by Charles Rennie Mackintosh. It was briefly an arts centre and is now used by Glasgow Social Services.

Buchanan Street and around → *For listings, see pages 59-85.*

Glasgow's commercial heart is the area between Buchanan Square and the M8. This vast grid-plan, home to the city's main shopping streets, businesses and financial institutions, inspired town planners in the USA. It is also where you'll find many of its architectural treasures.

At the bottom end of Buchanan Street is St Enoch Square, dominated by the **St Enoch Centre**, a gigantic glass-covered complex of shops, fast-food outlets and an ice rink. There's also a subway station and transport centre in the square. St Enoch Square looks onto **Argyle Street**, one of Glasgow's most famous shopping streets. Though its status has been usurped in recent decades by the more fashionable streets to the north, it does boast the **Argyle Arcade**, Scotland's first ever indoor-shopping mall, built in 1827 in Parisian style, at the junction with Buchanan Street.

Argyle Street runs west from here under the railway bridge at **Central station**. The bridge has always been known as the 'Heilanman's Umbrella', owing to the local joke that Highlanders would stand under it for shelter rather than buy an umbrella.

A short walk north on Buchanan Street is **Princes Square**, one of the most stylish and imaginative shopping malls in Britain. Even if you're not buying or looking, it's worth going in to admire this beautifully ornate art nouveau creation, or to sit at a top-floor café and watch others spend their hard-earned cash in the trendy designer clothes shops below. A little further north, on the opposite side of the street, is a branch of the famous **Willow Tea Rooms**, with replicas of Mackintosh designs. Almost opposite is a huge retail space – currently occupied by **All Saints** – housed in the huge and impressive former Royal Bank of Scotland (1827), which backs onto Royal Exchange Square.

The Lighthouse
ⓘ *11 Mitchell La, T0141-221 6362, www.thelighthouse.co.uk, Mon-Sat 1030-1700, Sun 1200-1700, free.*

Lovers of architecture should head west into Gordon Street and then south (left) into Mitchell Street, where you'll find The Lighthouse, a tardis-like building full of surprises. It was designed by the ubiquitous Charles Rennie Mackintosh in 1893 to house the offices of the *Glasgow Herald*. The *Herald* vacated the premises in 1980 and it lay empty, until its transformation into **Scotland's Centre for Architecture, Design and the City**, a permanent legacy of the Glasgow's role as UK City of Architecture and Design in 1999. The Lighthouse offers a programme of lively temporary exhibitions associated with architecture and design. This stunning 21st-century building also contains the **Mackintosh Interpretation and Review Gallery** on the third floor, which features original designs and information on the life and work of the great architect. There are interactive displays telling the story of his life and scale models of his works. From this gallery you can reach the **Mackintosh Viewing Tower**. Reached by a 135-step helical staircase, it was part of the original building and offers unbeatable, panoramic views of the city. There's also a viewing platform on Level 6 accessed via a lift. Two shops sell design pieces and Toshie goods echoing Mackintosh motifs and colour palette. The **Doocot** café bar on the fifth floor is a wonderful place to grab a light snack and relax.

Buchanan Street north and St Vincent Street
Further north on Buchanan Street, close to Buchanan Street Underground, are two more interesting buildings: St George's Tron Church, designed in 1808 by William Stark and the

Glasgow's Gaudí

To say that Barcelona has Gaudí and Glasgow has Rennie Mackintosh is not overstating the case. He is not only one of Scotland's most celebrated architects, but one of the creative geniuses of modern architecture.

Charles Rennie Mackintosh was born in Glasgow in 1868 and at 15 began work as a draughtsman with a local firm of architects. At the same time, he continued to pursue his studies at the Glasgow School of Art where his talent as an artist soon earned him recognition, and his experimental, decorative style brought him into contact with kindred spirits Herbert MacNair and two sisters, Frances and Margaret MacDonald. They became known as 'The Four' and together they developed their unique form of art and design, which became known as the 'Glasgow Style'.

Mackintosh was as much an artist and interior designer as an architect but he saw no conflict in this. He considered architecture to be "…the synthesis of the fine arts, the commune of all the crafts", and he used his diverse talents to great effect, designing every detail of a building, down to furniture, carpets and decoration. This can be seen to greatest effect in his most important building, the Glasgow School of Art.

In the late 1890s he began his Argyle Street tea room project for Miss Cranston, and developed his distinctive, elegant high-backed chairs, for which he is probably best known today. In 1900 he married Margaret Macdonald (Herbert MacNair and Margaret's sister were married the previous year) and they began to design the interior of their own flat, creating their distinctive colour schemes of white and grey, pink and purple, and the light and dark interiors representing the masculine and feminine.

Throughout his career, Mackintosh's talents were far better understood abroad than at home, where his designs were often criticized as being iconoclastic and too modern. He was forced to leave Glasgow in 1914 due to lack of work and soon became depressed and alcoholic, and though his fortunes improved after moving to London, he died, a tragic but romantic figure, in 1928.

It is only in the past few decades that his genius has been fully recognized and serious efforts made to preserve his artistic legacy. The restoration of the Willow Tea Rooms, Scotland Street School, Queen's Cross Church and the Mackintosh House at the Hunterian Art Gallery, as well as The Hill House in Helensburgh, are all testimony to his prodigious talents.

oldest church in the city centre, and the Athenaeum, designed in 1886 by JJ Burnet and showing early signs of his later modernism.

Running west from George Square, between Argyle Street and Sauchiehall Street, is St Vincent Street, where you'll find some extraordinary buildings. At No 78 is the **Phoenix Assurance building** (1913) in American neo-classical style; **The Hatrack**, at No 142-144 and designed in 1902 by James Salmon Junior, is a tall, narrow red-sandstone beauty with stained glass and a fantastically detailed roof resembling an old hat stand; and the elegant **Royal Alliance Building** (1929) at No 200 has an angular art deco statue added in the 1930s.

Further along St Vincent Street at No 256, near the intersection with Pitt Street, is one of the jewels in Glasgow's architectural crown, **St Vincent Street Church** ① T141-221 1937, www.glasgowcityfreechurch.org, contact the church office to arrange a tour, designed in 1859 by Alexander 'Greek' Thomson (1817-1875), the city's 'unknown genius' of architecture.

Much of his work was destroyed in the 1960s and this is his only intact Romantic Classical church, now on the World Monument Fund's list of the 100 most endangered sites. The Presbyterian church is fronted by Ionic columns like those of a Greek temple and the church also shows Egyptian and Assyrian decoration. The main tower is Grecian in style while the dome could have come straight out of India during the Raj. It was added to the World Monument Watch for endangered buildings in the 90s.

A series of streets climb northwards from St Vincent Street up to Sauchiehall Street, another of the city's main shopping thoroughfares. If there's one thing Glaswegians like to do it's spend money and Glasgow is second only to London in the UK in terms of retail spending. The upmarket shopping centre called the **Buchanan Galleries**, next door to the **Royal Concert Hall**, see page 76, is at the north end of Buchanan Street, where it meets the east end of Sauchiehall Street.

Sauchiehall Street and around → *For listings, see pages 59-85.*

There are a few notable places of interest here, including Charles Rennie Mackintosh's wonderful **Willow Tea Rooms** ⓘ *No 217, above Henderson's the Jewellers, www.willowtearooms.co.uk, 0900-1700, see also page 67.* This is a faithful reconstruction on the site of the original 1903 tea room, designed by CRM for his patron Miss Kate Cranston, who already ran three of the city's most fashionable tea rooms, in Argyle Street, Buchanan Street and Ingram Street. The tea room was very much peculiar to Glasgow, promoted by the Temperance Movement as a healthy alternative to the gin palaces, popular throughout the country in the late 19th century, and Miss Cranston's were the crème de la crème of tea rooms. They offered ladies-only rooms, rooms for gentlemen and rooms where both sexes could dine together. In addition, her tea rooms offered a reading room, a billiards room for the gentlemen and a smoking room, not forgetting the unrivalled splendour of the decoration. Mackintosh had already worked with Miss Cranston on her other tea rooms, but Sauchiehall Street was their tour de force. Sauchiehall means 'alley of the willows' and this theme was reflected not only in the name, but throughout the interior. Mackintosh was allowed free rein to design the fixtures and fittings; everything, in fact, right down to the teaspoons. The exclusive Salon de Luxe, on the first floor, was the crowning glory, and the most exotic and ambitious part of the tea rooms, decorated in purple, silver and white, with silk and velvet upholstery. Visitors today can relive the splendour of the original tea rooms as they relax in the distinctive high-backed chairs with a cup of tea, brought to them by the specially selected high-backed waitresses.

Further down the street, on the same side, the **Centre for Contemporary Arts (CCA)** ⓘ *T0141-352 4900, www.cca-glasgow.com, centre Mon-Sat 1000-2400, galleries Mon-Sat 1100-1800, free,* is housed in the Grecian Buildings, a former commercial warehouse designed by Alexander 'Greek' Thomson in 1867-1868. The centre presents six art shows a year featuring international contemporary artists. There's also a changing programme of contemporary theatre, dance, cinema, music and other cultural events. A light-filled courtyard ambience can be enjoyed under the glass canopy of the excellent **Saramango Café Bar**. For art books check out their superb shop.

Glasgow School of Art

ⓘ *167 Renfrew St, T0141-353 4526, www.gsa.ac.uk, visitor centre 1000-1830, guided tours generally 1100, 1300, 1500 and 1700 (contact for latest schedule: booking advised), closed late Jun for graduation and Christmas to New Year, £10, students £8. Entry to the school is by guided tour only which visits the main rooms containing many of the well-known pieces of furniture. It is still a working art school, so take note of the annual holidays when it's closed.*

Barcelona has the Sagrada Familia, New York the Empire State Building and Glasgow has its School of Art. A very steep walk up from Sauchiehall Street is the city's defining monument, and one of the most prestigious art schools in the country. The building was designed by Charles Rennie Mackintosh, after his proposal won a competition set to find a design for the school, in 1896. It was built in two stages from 1897-1899 and completed in 1907.

Much of the inspiration for his design came from nature and from his drawings of traditional Scottish buildings. He was also influenced by the art nouveau style, particularly the illustrations of Aubrey Beardsley. The school is now regarded as Mackintosh's architectural masterpiece and gives full expression to his architectural ideals. It is rooted in tradition, with a thoroughly modern-looking exterior of extreme austerity, and there

More Mackintosh

Aside from the Mackintosh buildings listed separately, there are a number of his lesser known works scattered around the city centre.

These include the former **Daily Record Building** (1901), at 20-26 Renfield Lane (external viewing only); the **Royal Fusiliers Museum** (circa 1903), at 518 Sauchiehall Street (ring for opening times, T0141-332 0961); **Ruchill Church Hall**, Shakespeare Street (open from Monday to Friday 1030-1430, closed July and August, free); and the former **Glasgow Society of Lady Artists' Club** (1908), at 5 Blythswood Square (external viewing only).

are medieval, castle-like features such as turrets and curving stairwells. The interior is both spacious and utilitarian and shows perfectly his desire to create a unified and harmonious working environment for both students and teachers. The studio walls and high ceilings are painted white, with huge windows allowing light to pour into the spaces. The corridors and staircases are decorated with glazed coloured tiles to help guide students and staff around the massive building. In the famous two-storey library Mackintosh also designed the light fittings, bookcases and the oak furniture. There are symbols of nature everywhere throughout the building, used to inspire the students to produce their own works of art. And who could fail to be inspired in such a stunning environment?

Tenement House

① *144 Buccleuch St, T0844-493 2197, www.nts.org.uk, 1 Mar-31 Oct, 1300-1700, £6.50, concession £5.*

A few hundred yards northwest of the School of Art, down the other side of the hill, is the Tenement House, a typical late Victorian tenement flat built in 1892. This was the home of Miss Agnes Toward, a shorthand typist, for 50 years until she moved out in 1965. It's a fascinating time-capsule of life in the first half of the 20th century and retains most of the original features such as the bed recesses, kitchen range and coal bunker. The whole experience is a little voyeuristic, as the flat includes many of Agnes' personal possessions, and in the parlour the table is set for afternoon tea, lending a spooky atmosphere redolent of the Marie Celeste. On the ground floor is an exhibition on tenement life.

On the other side of Cowcaddens Road, behind the huge Royal Scottish Academy for Music and Drama, is the National Piping Centre.

National Piping Centre

① *30-34 McPhater St, T0141-353 0220, www.thepipingcentre.co.uk, Mon-Fri 0900-1700, Sat 1000-1300, £4.50, concession £3.50.*

This is the national centre for the promotion of the bagpipes, which contains rehearsal rooms, performance spaces and accommodation for aficionados of an instrument that divides opinion sharply. There's also a very fine café, and a museum which features a collection of antique pipes and assorted artefacts. Pride of place goes to the chanter of Iain Dall (Blind John) MacKay (1650-1740), the oldest surviving chanter of the Highland bagpipe anywhere. There are audio visual displays and headsets so you can listen bagpipe music as you go round. Book a Tour and Try visit that allows visitors to blow a lungful and extract some overtones.

West End → *For listings, see pages 59-85.*

On the other side of the M8 is the West End, an area which contains many of the city's major museums, as well some of its finest examples of Victorian architecture. It's populated mostly by students and is full of fashionable shops, bars, cafés and restaurants. During the course of the 19th century the West End grew in importance as wealthy merchants moved here, away from the dirt and grime of the industrial city. By the middle of the 19th century the **Park Conservation Area** had been established and was described as one of the finest pieces of architectural planning of the century. Perhaps the most impressive of all the terraces in the conservation area are **Park Quadrant** and **Park Terrace**, with glorious views across **Kelvingrove Park**. Soon after, in 1870, the **university** also moved west, to its present site overlooking Kelvingrove Park, and in 1896 the Glasgow District Subway was extended west. In 1888 the park was used to stage an international exhibition and the profits were used to build the magnificent **Kelvingrove Art Gallery and Museum** which housed the second international exhibition in 1901. The bustling hub of the West End is Byres Road, running south from the Great Western Road past Hillhead Underground. Named after a small *clachan* (village) its cobbled lanes – Cresswell, Ruthven and most notably Ashton Lane – retain the rustic past and adds some alternative contemporary culture with independent restaurants, bars and shops; see pages 68, 74 and 80.

Mitchell Street Library

ⓘ *North St, T0141-287 2999, www.glasgowlife.org.uk, Mon-Thu 0900-200, Fri-Sat 0900-1700, free.*

Above the M8 motorway traffic din hovers a green dome topped with a statue of Minerva, belonging to the largest public reference library in Europe. This place of wisdom and learning is the wonderful legacy of the tobacco heir Stephen Mitchell – whose bust is in the entrance hall. The collection moved to its present site in 1911. Walk around the building to view sculpted figures of artistic luminaries including Beethoven, Michelangelo and Mozart. Take a look inside, say hello to one of the amiable janitors and explore the handsome marble and dark wood-lined corridors. Upstairs are corridors with kitsch 1970s geometric carpets and many reading rooms. The Family History Section helps people from all around the world to explore the rich archive sources and delve into the past. Literary and artistic events – including the Aye Write Literature Festival in March – are staged here. Take a break in the sleek new **Herald Café Bar**, which has a terrace next to the nearby Mitchell Theatre.

Approaching Kelvingrove Park via Park Circus

Heading north from Mitchell Street library and the roaring M8 are some leafy streets lined with some fine architecture. At the junction of Woodlands Road and Woodlands Gate (opposite the **Halt Bar**) is a humorous statue of pint-sized sheriff Lobey Dosser and handcuffed villain Rank Bajin astride two-legged steed El Fideldo, sculpted by visionary artist Tony Morrow and Nick Gillon. It's said to be the world's lone two-legged – by design – equestrian monument. There's a plaque honouring Bud Neill who created the popular late 1940s-50s cartoon strip character of Calton Creek. Follow the elegant Victorian terraces around **Park Circus** – designed by Charles Wilson (1810-1863) – to the entrance of **Kelvingrove Park**, the site of three International Exhibitions (1888, 1901 and 1911), Glasgow's high-profile contributions to the British Empire. It was originally opened as the West End Park, and was created by English gardener Sir Joseph Paxton in 1852 around the

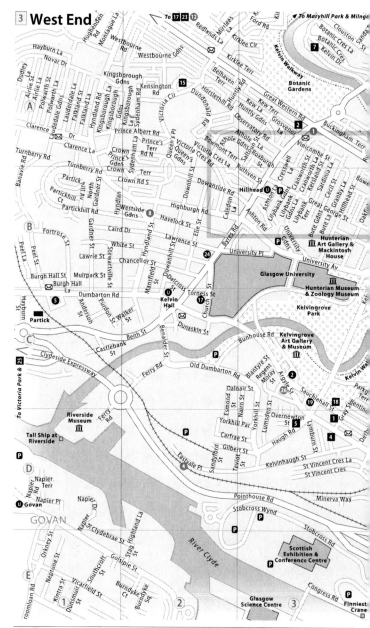

➡ **Glasgow maps**
1 Glasgow, page 22
2 Glasgow centre, page 26
3 West End, page 40
4 Byres Road detail, page 42

N

200 metres
200 yards

Where to stay

Argyll **1** *D3*
Cairncross House **4** *D3*
City Apartments **3** *B5*
Dreamhouse Inc **6** *C5*
Embassy
 Apartments **7** *A3*
Hilton Glasgow
 Grosvenor **2** *A3*
Hotel du Vin **17** *A2*
Kelvinhaugh Gate **5** *D3*
Kirklee **15** *A2*
Manor Park **25** *C1*
Sandyford **18** *C3*
SYHA Youth Hostel **19** *C4*
White House **23** *A2*

Restaurants

Ashoka West End **2** *C3*
Balbir's **17** *C2*
Bay Tree **3** *B5*
Butchershop **19** *C3*
Cabin **5** *C1*
Grassroots Café **10** *C5*
La Parmigiana **13** *B4*
Mother India **14** *D4*
Mr Singh's India **15** *D5*
North Star **23** *A4*
Shish Mahal **20** *B4*
Stravaigin **21** *B4*
Two Fat Ladies
 at the Buttery **28** *E5*
University Café **24** *B2*

Bars & clubs

Black Sparrow **7** *D5*
Cottier's **8** *B2*
Dram! **30** *C5*
Firebird **26** *C3*
Halt Bar **27** *C5*
Lock 27 **12** *A2*
Òran Mór **1** *A3*
SWG3 & Poetry Club **4** *D2*

banks of the River Kelvin. An impressive statue of Field Marshal Earl Roberts of Kandahar (1832-1914) guards the entrance while the east end of the Prince of Wales bridge is marked by a memorial to the men of the Highland Light Infantry who fell in the Boer War (1899-1902). The largest moument is the **Stewart Memorial Fountain** (undergoing refurbishment), a tribute to the Lord Provost who secured a water supply to the city from Loch Katrine. Also of note is the **bandstand** built in 1924, closed in 1999 due to vandalism and set for a reprieve through a repair grant. Bands and theatre performances are due to return to this much-loved Glasgow outdoor venue with amphitheatre seating.

Kelvingrove Art Gallery and Museum

ⓘ *Argyle St, T0141-276 9599, www.glasgowmuseums.com, Mon-Thu and Sat 1000-1700, Fri and Sun 1100-1700, free. Bus 9, 16, 23, 42 and 62; Kelvinhall subway station is 5 mins' walk away.*

At the western edge of the park rises the red-sandstone Victorian grandeur of the Kelvingrove, built between 1891 and 1901, opened as the Palace of Fine Arts for the International Exhibition of 1901. It houses a world-class civic collection now visited by over a million people each year. The city's art collection has its origins in the paintings of Trades House Deacon Convenor Archibald McLellan, which was acquired with the Sauchiehall Street gallery in 1854. After the roaring success of the much-visited 1888 International Exhibition – attended by Queen Victoria and 6 million of her subjects – a project was conceived to build this colossal building to house the collection. Its twin towers shelter a

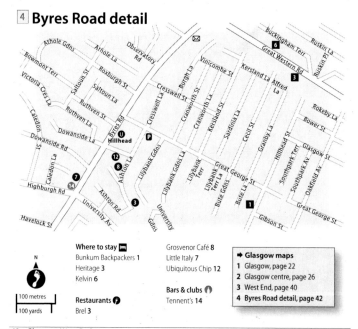

4 Byres Road detail

Where to stay 🛏
Bunkum Backpackers **1**
Heritage **3**
Kelvin **6**

Restaurants 🍴
Brel **3**
Grosvenor Café **8**
Little Italy **7**
Ubiquitous Chip **12**

Bars & clubs 🍷
Tennent's **14**

➡ **Glasgow maps**
1 Glasgow, page 22
2 Glasgow centre, page 26
3 West End, page 40
4 Byres Road detail, page 42

100 metres
100 yards

Kids might like...

The West End has fabulous attractions for families with children. Green spaces include the Kelvingrove Park and the Botanic Gardens and there are leafy walks along the River Kelvin. Stimulate young minds at the Kelvingrove Art Gallery and Museum, which is full of natural and artistic wonders, and organizes special tours and activities for all ages. Head to the Clyde to explore engines, aeroplanes and Glasgow's historic streets at the futuristic Riverside Museum, then hop aboard the Tall Ship berthed outside, or take a boat trip *doon the watter*.

massive bronze statue of St Mungo facing the lacework spire of Glasgow University. The parkland side has a grand staircase leading to sunken gardens.

The collection includes over 8000 objects over three floors, 22 themed galleries and family-friendly interactive displays. Among the fabulous works of art are masterpieces of the Italian Renaissance, French Impressionism, post-Impressionism and 17th-century Dutch and Flemish portraiture. Standout works include Botticelli's *Annunciation*, Rembrandt's *Man in Armour* and Dali's *Christ of St John*. A recent three-year refurbishment costing £27.9 million restored its treasures, upgraded facilities and has made it more popular than ever with Glasgwegians and visitors alike. The West Court has been transformed with dynamic displays including a hanging Spitfire LA68. Discovery Centres are dedicated to art, environment and history. Young people aged 10-14 can go on educational adventures in the **Centre of New Enlightenment** ⓘ *T0141-276 9544*. There's an excellent gift shop and a buzzing café-restaurant in the basement.

Kelvin Walkway

The Kelvin Walkway follows the River Kelvin from Kelvingrove Park through the northwest of the city to Dawsholm Park, about three miles away. It goes through the Botanic Gardens and under the Forth and Clyde Canal. With the appropriate maps you could follow one waterway out and return by the other. The path starts just west of the Kelvin Hall, by the bridge on the Dumbarton Road.

Glasgow University and the Hunterian Museum

ⓘ *University Av, T0141-330 4221, www.hunterian.gla.ac.uk, Tue-Sat 1000-1700, Sun 1100-1600, free.*

The university's roots go back to 1451 when Pope Nicholas V authorized William Turnbull, Bishop of Glasgow, to found a seat of learning in the city. At first there was just an arts faculty and lectures were held in the cathedral crypt and neighbouring monastery. In the 17th century the university moved to new premises in the High Street, but these became too small and, in 1870, it moved to its present site, on Gilmorehill, overlooking Kelvingrove Park. The Gothic buildings were designed by Sir George Gilbert Scott, though the Lion and Unicorn balustrade on the stone staircase opposite the Principal's Lodging is a relic of the old High Street colleges, as is the stonework of the lodge gateway. The ornate **Bute Hall**, which is now used for graduation and other ceremonies, was added in 1882. The **university chapel** is also worth seeing. The starting point of a tour is the **University Visitor Centre**, near the main gate, which features interactive displays on the university and a coffee bar.

Contained within the university buildings is the Hunterian Museum, named after William Hunter (1718-1783), a student at the university in the 1730s. His bequest to the university of his substantial collections led to the establishment of the Hunterian Museum in 1807, Scotland's oldest public museum. It has displays of social history, archaeology and geology, and includes Roman relics from the Antonine Wall and one of the largest coin collections in Britain. Highlights include dinosaur's eggs, artefacts from Captain Cook's voyages and the death mask of the collection's brainchild. There's also a **Zoology Museum** ① *Mon-Sat 0900-1700*, housed in the Graham Kerr Building, a few minutes' walk from the main museum. The **Anatomy Collection** ① *by appointment only*, shows Hunter's pioneering work as an anatomist and obstetrician; it's housed very near the Hunterian in the Thomson Building towards Kelvin Way.

Hunterian Art Gallery and Mackintosh House
① *T0141-330 4221, www.hunterian.gla.co.uk, Tue-Sat 100-1700, Sun 1100-1600, free. Buses 44 and 44A from the city centre (Hope St), or the Underground to Hillhead and walk.*
Opposite the University is the Hunterian Art Gallery, a modern building containing the more interesting part of Hunter's bequest, the fabulous art collection. The gallery holds an important collection of European paintings including works by Rembrandt, Koninck, Rubens, Pissaro, and Rodin, as well as 18th-century British portraits by Ramsay and Reynolds. There is also a fine collection of Scottish 19th- and 20th-century paintings including works by McTaggart Guthrie and Fergusson. Indeed this is a superb place to explore the work of the Scottish Colourists and groundbreaking style of the Glasgow Boys; see box, opposite. Arguably the big draw is the impressive collection of works by the American painter, James McNeill Whistler. There are some 70 paintings and a selection of his personal possessions (including his specially made long-handled paintbrushes) on show, making it the largest display of his work outside the USA. Among the works are many of his distinctive full-length portraits and some moody depictions of the Thames.

Attached to the gallery is the **Mackintosh House**, a stunning reconstruction of the main interiors from 78 Southpark Avenue, the Glasgow home of Charles Rennie Mackintosh and his wife, Margaret MacDonald, from 1906 to 1914. A stairway leads to an introductory display containing numerous drawings and designs, including those for his major buildings, furniture and interiors. From there you are led into the cool, soothing rooms, lovingly reconstructed and exquisitely furnished with some 80 original pieces of his furniture. These provide the perfect example of just why this innovative designer and architect is so revered. Among the highlights are: the Studio Drawing Room, decorated in white and flooded with natural light, and the guest bedroom from Northampton, a later commission, with its bold and dazzling geometric designs. When George Bernard Shaw, a guest, was asked if the decor would disturb his sleep, he replied, "No, I always sleep with my eyes closed."

Botanic Gardens
① *730 Great Western Rd, T0141-276 1614, www.glasgowbotanicgardens.com, 0700 till dusk, free, Kibble Palace and all glasshouses open daily 1000-1800 in summer, 1000-1615 in winter, Tearooms 1000-1615 in summer, 1000-dusk winter.*
At the top of Byres Road, where it meets the Great Western Road, is the entrance to the Botanic Gardens, a smallish but perfectly formed park where you can lose yourself along the remote paths that follow the wooded banks of the River Kelvin. They were created to provide medical and botanical students at the university with fresh plant material, but soon became a fashionable place to promenade. There are two large hothouses in the park, one of which is the **Kibble Palace** built as a conservatory for the Clyde Coast home

Glasgow Boys

With the coming of the industrial age, Glasgow had grown rapidly from a small, provincial town into the 'Second City of the Empire'. This sudden growth in size and wealth led to the beginnings of the famous and long-standing rivalry between Glasgow and Edinburgh, and, by the 1880s, to a new departure from the cultural mainstream, when a group of students nicknamed the Glasgow Boys, united in protest against Edinburgh's dominance of the arts.

This group of five painters – Guthrie, Hornel, Lavery, Henry and Crawhall – rejected the traditional concept of art which was confined to historical melodrama, sentimental 'poor but happy' cottagers and grandiose visions of the Highlands inspired by Sir Walter Scott. They referred to these paintings as 'gluepots' for their use of megilp, a treacly varnish that lent the paintings a brown patina of age. Instead, they experimented with colour and, inspired by the European Realists, chose earthy, peasant themes. This not only shocked and offended the genteel Edinburgh art establishment, but also scandalized their fellow citizens.

The Glasgow Boys left Scotland to study in Paris, where their work met with great acclaim. Subsequently their art began to fetch high prices from the new rich of Glasgow, eager to buy status through cultural patronage. But once the group had achieved the artistic respect and commercial success its members craved, they sadly lost their freshness.

The influence of the Glasgow Boys cannot be underestimated. They shook the foundations of the art establishment and were the inspiration for the next generation of great Scottish painters, known as the 'Colourists'.

of Glasgow businessman and eccentric, John Kibble, and then shipped to its present site in 1873. It was once used for public meetings and British prime ministers William Gladstone and Benjamin Disraeli both gave their rectorial addresses here when they became rectors of the university. The **domed glasshouse**, contains the national collection of tree ferns and temperate plants from around the world. The **main glasshouse** is more attractive, and has 11 sections featuring plants such as cacti, palms, insectivorous plants and palms. Its collections of orchids and begonias are outstanding. There is also a herb garden with five beds growing medicinal, culinary, dye and scented plants. The central bed has plants that have been used in the past in Scotland. Look out for meadowsweet, used for headaches; coltsfoot used for coughs and chest complaints, and yellow flag iris – the leaves of which give a bright green dye and the rhizomes a black dye which were traditionally used in the Harris tweed industry. In the Outer Hebrides the black dye was used for the cloth for the suits worn on Sundays. Kibble Palace and the grounds host cultural events – art shows, talks, music and theatre – as well as book fairs.

Just over the road from the Botanic Gardens is the imposing Kelvinside Parish Church, converted recently into the Òran Mór arts and entertainment centre, see page 77.

Queen's Cross Church

ⓘ *870 Garscube Rd, T0141-946 6600, www.crmsociety.com, Mon, Wed and Fri 1000-1700, Sun Mar-Oct 1400-1700, £4, concession £2. Buses 40 and 61 from Hope St, or Underground to St George's Cross and walk 15 mins along Cronwell St and Maryhill Rd.*
This is the only church owned by the Charles Rennie Mackintosh Society and a fascinating piece of architecture. It's beautifully simple, with dramatic use of light and space that

echoes in the symbolism of his other buildings. Highlights include beautiful stained glass and relief carving on wood and stonework. It is now the headquarters of the CRM society, with an excellent library and a shop brimming with Mackintosh books and gifts.

Along the Clyde → *For listings, see pages 59-85.*

Riverside Museum: Scotland's Museum of Transport and Travel

ⓘ *100 Pointhouse Place, T0141-287 2720, www.glasgowmuseums.com, Mon-Thu and Sat 1000-1700, Fri and Sun 1100-1700, free. Bus no 100 from George Sq, subway to Kelvinhall or Partick then 10-min walk, limited pay and display parking £1 up to 4 hrs.*

A striking addition to the Clyde waterfront regeneration, the Riverside opened as the new home of Glasgow's much-loved Museum of Transport collection in 2011. Zaha Hadid's zig-zag heartbeat-monitor profile, expanse of glass and pleated roof recalling a muscular engine is meant to be a nod to Clydeside industry. Indeed inside feels like a covered workshop – filled floor to cylinder-like ceiling with oily trappings of transport. A greenish-yellow colour scheme, swanky café and interactive displays make for a more contemporary experience compared to the darker old museum at Kelvin Hall. Eye-catching displays include a Wall of Cars, The Rest and Be Thankful Road of classic cars, Hanging Bicycle Velodrome and Motorbike Deck. Pride of place goes to the ship *Patternoster* displaying the world-famous collection of Clyde-built ship models. From the bridge you can survey planes, trains, cars and bikes shooting out in all directions. Riveting exhibits include: the 150-tonne South African Locomotive 3007 built in Glasgow in 1944-1945; Argyll Motors' handsome coach-built cars; a 1924 Bugatti Type T; Disco Dave's Number 10 Peace camp caravan; the first Hillman Imp; and a replica glider by flight pioneer Percy Pilcher. Kelvin Street now consists of three street displays spanning the years 1895-1930, 1930-1960 and 1960-1980s. Main Street brings the past to life with fixtures and fittings of Mitre Bar, Le Rendezvous Café, pawnbroker, a funeral parlour and subway station with train. Riverside's café terrace and plaza is the focus of events and concerts, and overlooks the ship *Glenlee* (see below). Seasonal ferries now ply the Clyde stopping at Riverside including the **Govan Ferry** (£3 return), **Braehead Ferry** (see Clyde Cruises, page 81) and occasional speciality trips; check the website for latest trips and events. It's a 20-minute walk along the River Kelvin footpath near Kelvingrove and then Ferry Road.

Tall Ship at Riverside

ⓘ *100 Pointhouse Quay, T0800-328 1373, www.thetallship.com, Mar-Oct daily 1000-1700, Nov-Feb daily 1000-1600, £5, concession £4.50.*

Moored alongside the Riverside Museum is the handsome sailing ship, the *SS Glenlee* otherwise known as the Tall Ship. Launched in 1896, this 245-ft-long three-masted bald-headed rig was built on the Clyde and is one of only five Clyde-built sailing ships that remain afloat in the world. She circumnavigated the globe four times and carried cargo as varied as coal, grain and even guano, which was transported from Chile to the European ports of Antwerp and Rotterdam to be used as fertilizer. The ammonia fumes from the guano were so pungent they corroded the lining of sailors' noses and even killed the occasional ship's cat. The *Glenlee* was saved from a Seville scrapyard in 1992 and has now been restored. Exhibitions on board provide a vivid insight into the daily lives of the sailors and the conditions on board ship in 1896.

A fishy tale

Though it is many years since salmon were caught in the Clyde, two appear in the city's coat of arms. Each fish has a ring in its mouth, recalling an old local legend.

The Queen of Strathclyde was given a ring by her husband but then promptly gave it to her lover. The king found the lover wearing the ring as he slept beside the Clyde. He took the ring and threw it into the water, and then went to his wife and asked her to show it to him. The Queen prayed to St Mungo for help, and immediately, one of her servants miraculously found the ring in the mouth of a salmon he had caught. The king then had to accept his wife's pleas of innocence, despite knowing something fishy was going on.

Glasgow Science Centre and around

ⓘ *50 Pacific Quay, T0141-420 5000, www.gsc.org.uk, Science Mall Apr-Oct daily 1000-1700, Nov-Mar Wed-Fri 1000-1300, Sat and Sun 1000-1700, £10, concession £8, add-ons to visit another attraction including IMAX feature £2.50. Buses 23, 26 and 90 go to the Science Centre from the city centre.*

The £75 million Glasgow Science Centre opened late in 2001 on the south side of the Clyde on the former garden festival site. This enormous complex aims to demystify science, bringing it life with imaginative displays and interactive exhibits covering everything from the human body to the internet. The kids love it – as do their parents.

The heart of the centre is the **Science Mall**, with three floors of themed exhibits. The first floor looks at how we experience the world, the second floor looks at science in action and the third floor looks at how science affects your daily life. You can find anything here from laboratories where you can study your own skin or hair through a microscope, to an infra-red harp which you play with a beam of light.

Glasgow Tower, the tallest free-standing building in Scotland at 127 m, has experienced some engineering problems and at the time of writing it was shut for renovation works. At the top there's a viewing cabin with superb views over Glasgow and the Clyde. The centre also contains an IMAX theatre with Scotland's largest screen and state-of-the-art sound system.

Opposite the Science Centre is the **Scottish Exhibition and Conference Centre** (**SECC**), which was built in 1987 on the site of the former Queen's Dock. Next door is the **Clyde Auditorium** known locally as the 'Armadillo', which was designed by Sir Norman Foster and built in 1997. It's used as a venue for major pop and rock acts and as a business and conference centre.

Clyde Walkway

The Clyde Walkway is a 40-mile walking route designed to link the centre of Glasgow to the Falls of Clyde at Lanark, via the Clyde Valley, see page 56. Sections of the waterfront walk are still rather empty and depressing but the central part, between Victoria Bridge and the SECC, is interesting and takes in some of the more distinguished bridges and much of Glasgow's proud maritime heritage.

Start the walk at **Victoria Bridge**, built in 1854 to replace the 14th-century Old Glasgow Bridge, and continue past the graceful **Suspension Bridge**, built in 1851 as a grand entrance to the 'new town' on the south bank. You can cross from here to **Carlton Place** whose impressive Georgian façades have been restored and which were designed

Other walkways and country jaunts

Kelvin Walkway ⓘ *see page 43*, follows the River Kelvin from Kelvingrove Park through the northwest of the city to Dawsholm Park, about three miles away.

The **Forth and Clyde Canal** ⓘ *route information is available from T0141-332 6936, www.scottishcanals.co.uk*, was opened in 1790 and provided a convenient short-cut for trading ships between Northern Europe and North America, linking both coasts of Scotland. The towpath starts at Port Dundas, just north of the M8 by Craighall Road, and runs to the main canal at the end of Lochburn Road, off Maryhill road. It then runs east all the way to Kirkintilloch and Falkirk, and west, through Maryhill and Drumchapel to Bowling and the River Clyde. It passes through sections of bleak industrial wasteland, but there are many interesting sights along the way and open, rural stretches.

At **Mugdock Country Park** ⓘ *see page 53*, in the select suburb of Milngavie, you can pretend that you're in the country as there are over 300 ha of unspoilt grounds and ancient woodlands to explore. It's open from dawn to dusk every day.

Other country parks with walks and nature trails are **Clyde Muirshiel Park** ⓘ *Lochwinnoch, T01505-614 791, www.clydemuirshiel.co.uk, 30 mins' drive from the centre*. It covers 102 square miles of land and has walks in woods and over moorland. Also here is an **RSPB Nature Reserve** ⓘ *T01505-842663, www.rspb. org.uk/reserves/guide/l/lochwinnoch*, with feeding stations and nature trails for the family.

A Glasgow–Edinburgh route incorporates part of the Clyde Walkway. The West Highland Way begins in Milngavie, eight miles north of the city centre, and runs for 95 miles to Fort William.

to front the never-completed 'new town'. Back on the north bank is **Customs House Quay** and, further west beyond George V Bridge, **Broomielaw Quay**. From here, Henry Bell's Comet inaugurated the world's first commercial passenger steamboat service. This was also the departure point for many Scottish emigrants to North America, and, later, for thousands of holidaying locals heading 'doon the watter' to the Firth of Clyde seaside resorts. Further west, at Anderston Quay, is the **PS Waverley Terminal**, home of the iconic paddle steamer rebuilt in 1946 – the original was sunk at Dunkirk in 1940 – and restored in 2000. Between jaunts around the British Isles she makes regular visits to the Clyde, especially during the summer months. Between here and the SECC is the huge 53-m-high **Finnieston Crane** which was once used for lifting railway locomotives at a time when Glasgow was the largest builder of these in the world outside North America. Close by is the **Rotunda** (1890-1896), once the northern terminal of the complex of tunnels which took horse traffic and pedestrians under the river, until the building of a new road tunnel in the 1960s. The Rotunda has been restored as a restaurant complex. Soon you come to the **Scottish Exhibition and Conference Centre** (SECC) and the **Clyde Auditorium** (known locally as the 'Armadillo'), sitting opposite the **Glasgow Science Centre** and **BBC Scotland HQ**, Pacific Quay. Returning to the northern shore you can walk to the **Riverside Museum** and **Tall Ship Glenlee** (see above).

Check online for latest programme of tours at the **BBC Scotland's HQ** ⓘ *Pacific Quay, T0141-422 6000, www.bbc.co.uk/showsandtours/tours*, which provide a fascinating insight into state-of-the-art broadcasting facilities, with studio visits and the chance to spot some celebs.

South Side → *For listings, see pages 59-85.*

South of the River Clyde is a part of Glasgow largely unknown to most visitors, except for two of the city's most notable attractions, the **Burrell Collection** and **Pollok House**, both set in the sylvan surrounds of Pollok Country Park. There are other reasons to venture south of the river, however, not least of these being to see Charles Rennie Mackintosh's **House for an Art Lover** in nearby Bellahouston Park. Further east is another stop on the Mackintosh trail, the **Scotland Street School Museum of Education**. At Pollockshields East is the fabulous **Tramway** arts centre. To the south, in Cathcart, is **Holmwood House**, Alexander 'Greek' Thomson's great architectural masterpiece. Further south brings more green pleasures at **Rouken Park** and **Greenbank Garden**.

Govan

Flanking the Clyde is Govan, forever associated with shipbuilding and not worth a trip, unless you're visiting Ibrox, home of Glasgow Rangers, or looking for **Govan Old Parish** ① *Church Govan Rd, near Govan Cross underground, T0141-440 2466, www.govanold.org.uk, daily worship Mon-Fri at 1000, Sun 1100 and 1830, at other times by appointment, free*. Not only does the church stand on an ancient Christian site, it also has a unique collection of carved stones dating back to the ninth and tenth centuries. Intriguing examples include a sarcophagus with fine carvings, free-standing crosses and a group of five enigmatic hogback monuments. There's also a collection of stained glass windows with related themes all commissioned by Dr John Macleod, who was Govan Parish Church Minister from 1875 to 1898.

Scotland Street School Museum of Education

① *225 Scotland St, T0141-287 0500, www.glasgowmuseums.com, Tue-Thu and Sat 1000-1700, Fri and Sun 1100-1700, free. Underground to Shields Rd, or buses 90 and 121 from the city centre.*
Directly opposite Shields Road Underground is another of Charles Rennie Mackintosh's great works, the Scotland Street School, which opened in 1906 and closed in 1979. The entire school has been preserved as a museum of education and is a wonderfully evocative experience. The school has been refurbished and includes an audio-visual theatre and computer activities for children. There's a collection of school memorabilia and reconstructed classrooms from Victorian times up to the 1960s, as well as changing rooms, a science room and headmaster's office.

This was the most modern of Mackintosh's buildings and is notable for its semi-cylindrical glass stair towers, the magnificent tiled entrance hall and his customary mastery of the interplay of light and space. There's also a shop and café, but don't worry, they don't serve authentic school food.

Burrell Collection

① *2060 Pollokshaws Rd, T0141-649 7151, www.glasgow.gov.uk, Mon-Thu and Sat 1000-1700, Fri and Sun 1100-1700, free. Buses 34, 45, and 57 from the city centre (Union St) pass the park gates on Pollokshaws Rd, from the gates it's a 10-min walk to the gallery or there's a twice hourly bus service; regular trains from Central station to Pollockshaws West station; or a taxi from the city centre costs £12.*
A few miles southwest of the city centre is Glasgow's top attraction and a must on any visit, the Burrell Collection, standing in the extensive wooded parklands of Pollok Country Park.

The magnificent collection contains some 8500 art treasures, donated to the city in 1944 by the shipping magnate, William Burrell (1861-1958) who sold his shipping interests in order to devote the remainder of his life to collecting art. He began collecting in the 1880s, and in 1917 bought Hutton Castle near Berwick-on-Tweed to house his collection. There it stayed, even after his bequest to the city, as he stipulated that all the works in his collection be housed in one building in a rural setting because he was concerned about the possible damage caused by the pollution that then blackened Glasgow. It wasn't until the Clean Air Act of the 1960s and the council's acquisition of Pollok Park that a suitable site was found and the modern, award-winning gallery could be built – with the £450,000 donated by Burrell. The building opened to the public in 1983.

The collection includes ancient Greek, Roman and Egyptian artefacts, a huge number of dazzling oriental art pieces and numerous works of medieval and post-medieval European art, including tapestries, silverware, textiles, sculpture and exquisitely lit stained glass. The tapestries are particularly fine and date from the late 15th and 16th centuries. There's also an impressive array of paintings by Rembrandt, Degas, Pissaro, Bellini, and Manet amongst many others. Look out for the Warwick Vase, an eight-tonne Roman marble piece found at Hadrian's Villa, Tivoli in 1771. Rodin's famous bronze sculpture *The Thinker* (one of 14 casts made from the original) is, like many film stars and TV personalities you've only seen in pictures, smaller than you expect in real life.

The gallery is a stunning work of simplicity and thoughtful design, which allows the visitor to enjoy the vast collection to the full. The large, floor-to-ceiling windows give sweeping views over the surrounding woodland and allow a flood of natural light to enhance the treasures on view. Some sections of the gallery are reconstructions of rooms from Hutton Castle and incorporated into the structure are carved stone Romanesque doors. There's also a café and restaurant on the lower ground floor.

Pollok House
ⓘ *T0844-493 2202, www.nts.org.uk, house daily 1000-1700, Apr-Oct £6.50, child/concession £5 and Nov-Mar free, entry to the park is from Pollokshaws Rd, or Haggs Rd if you're on foot, car parking is at the Burrell Collection.*

Also in Pollok Country Park, a 10-minute walk from the Burrell, is Pollok House, designed by William Adam and finished in 1752. This was once the home of the Maxwell family, who owned most of southern Glasgow until well into the last century. It contains one of the best collections of Spanish paintings in Britain, including works by Goya, El Greco and Murillo. There are also paintings by William Blake, as well as glass, silverware, porcelain and furniture. The most interesting part of the house are the servants' quarters downstairs, which give you a real insight into life 'below stairs' – with rows of bells waiting to summon servants to any part of the house. There's a good tea room in the old kitchens. If the weather's fine, the park is worth exploring. There are numerous trails through the woods and meadows and guided walks with the countryside rangers. There are two golf courses within the park grounds, as well as a herd of highland cattle.

Cyclists may enjoy the beautiful surroundings and trails at Pollok Country Park, including three mountain bike circuits of varying difficulties. It's reached via Routes 7 and 75 of the **National Cycle Network** ⓘ *www.sustrans.org.uk.*

House for an Art Lover
ⓘ *10 Dumbreck Rd, T0141-353 4770, www.houseforanartlover.co.uk, times vary due to private events so call or check website in advance: generally Mon,Tue and Thu 1000-1600, Wed and Sun*

1000-1100, Fri 1000-1430, Sat 1000-1230. £4.50, concession £3. Take the Underground to Ibrox station and walk (15 mins), or bus 38, 36, 54 or 9 from Bus stop 1 at Union St, near Queen St Station.
A short distance north of Pollok Park is Bellahouston Park, site of another place on the Charles Rennie Mackintosh trail, the House for an Art Lover. The building was designed in 1901 as an entry to a competition run by a German design magazine, the brief being to create a lavish country house for an art lover. The interior and exterior had to be a coherent work of art. Building never went ahead during Mackintosh's lifetime and it was not until 1989 that construction began following his original drawings. It was not completed until 1996, when it became a centre for Glasgow School of Art postgraduate students, though a number of rooms on the lower floor are open to the public. Mackintosh worked closely with his wife on the design of the house and there is distinctive evidence of her influence, especially in the exquisite Music Room with its elaborate symbolism, particularly the rose motif, which is used throughout. But though the detail is, as ever, intense, the overall effect is one of space and light. The exterior of the house is equally impressive and totally original. On the ground floor is an excellent café, which is popular with locals; see page 71.

Queen's Park and around

To the east of Pollok Country Park, by Pollokshaws Road, is Queen's Park, named after Mary, Queen of Scots, whose reign ended after defeat here, at the Battle of Langside, in 1568. A memorial outside the park marks the site of the battle. It's a pleasant place for a stroll and the views north across the city make it even more enjoyable.

Close by, in Mount Florida, is **Hampden Park**, home of Scottish football, the 2014 Commonwealth Games Track and Field venue, and housing the **Scottish National Football Museum** ① *T0141-616 6139, www.scottishfootballmuseum.com, Mon-Sat 1000-1700, Sun 1100-1700, £6, concession £3, tour of the stadium extra £4 (£7 if not visiting museum).* The museum describes the history of the game in Scotland. This may strike some as a rather masochistic idea given some of the more infamous and embarrassing episodes, but there have been highs (Wembley 1967, Lisbon 1969, Paris 2007) as well as lows (Argentina 1978, Faroe Islands 2002 and Cardiff 2004). The museum is very large and includes a huge range of football memorabilia, from medals and jerseys to teapots. It even has the minutes of the very first meeting of Scotland's first football club – dated 9 July 1867. You can also get a guided tour of Hampden Park. To get there, take a train to Mount Florida station from Central station (turn left out of station and head straight downhill till you see the stadium (there are no signs); alternatively buses 5, 7, 12, 31, 66 or 75 will take you there.

Holmwood House

① *61-63 Netherlee Rd, T0844-493 2204, www.nts.org.uk, late Mar to 31 Oct, Thu-Mon 1200-1700, but access may be restricted at certain times, phone in advance, £6.50, child/concession £5. Trains every 30 mins to Cathcart from Central station, or take a bus from the city centre to Cathcart bridge, turn left onto Rannon Road and walk 10 mins to gates.*
South of Queen's Park and Hampden, in Cathcart, is Holmwood House, designed by Alexander 'Greek' Thomson, Glasgow's greatest Victorian architect; see box, page 52. Holmwood was built for James Couper, a paper manufacturer, between 1857 and 1858 and is the most elaborate and sumptuously decorated of all the villas Thomson designed for well-to-do industrialists on the outskirts of Glasgow. It was rescued from decline by the National Trust for Scotland in 1994 and is well worth a visit.

The building is a work of genuine originality and has become a monument of international importance, as Thomson was the first modern architect to apply a

Alexander the Great

Alexander Thomson was the greatest architect of Victorian Glasgow, who did as much to shape the city as the famous Charles Rennie Mackintosh. In the middle of the 19th century, when the "Second City of the Empire" was a growing, dynamic place, he brought a distinctive flair to all manner of buildings: warehouses and commercial premises, terraces and tenements, suburban villas and some of the finest Romantic Classical churches in the world.

Despite his nickname he never visited Greece and was not a conventional Greek Classicist. In fact, he thought the architects of the Greek revival had failed "because they could not see through the material into the laws upon which that architecture rested. They failed to master their style, and so became its slaves". Instead, Thomson evolved a distinctive manner of building using a Greek style but in an unconventional way and incorporating modern inventions such as iron beams and plate glass. Thomson was struck by "the mysterious power of the horizontal element in carrying the mind away into space and into speculations on infinity". This dominance of horizontality has led to comparisons with Frank Lloyd Wright, though Thomson predates him by 40 years.

Thomson was a truly original and brilliant architect yet was shamefully neglected after his death in 1875. In the 1960s, in a frenzy of destruction, the city planners did their best to wipe out this man's amazing achievements completely. Finally, though, the city paid tribute to one of their most talented sons with a major exhibition about his work as part of the City of Architecture and Design year.

For more information on Alexander 'Greek' Thomson and his surviving buildings, see the tourist office's Glasgow architectural guide 1. The only building open to the public is Holmwood House, in Cathcart, see page 51.

Greek style to a free, asymmetrical composition. The house has features reminiscent of modernist Frank Lloyd Wright. Thomson designed everything in the house and conservation work has revealed very beautiful and elaborate stencilled decoration and friezes with Greek motifs. The best description of Holmwood comes from Thomas Gildard who wrote in 1888: "If architecture be poetry in stone-and-lime – a great temple an epic – this exquisite little gem, at once classic and picturesque, is as complete, self-contained and polished as a sonnet"

Glasgow is surrounded by a series of drab satellite towns, once major centres of coal and steel, or shipbuilding, which are struggling to recover their identity. It's tempting to pass through this depressed hinterland, especially as the delights of the West Highlands lie northwest just beyond the city's boundary, but there are some interesting sights for those with the time or the inclination. The 18th-century model community of **New Lanark** and the spectacular **Falls of Clyde** nearby are well worth the trip from Glasgow, and there are a couple of interesting historical sights near Hamilton, namely **Bothwell Castle** and **Chatelherault**.

Mugdock Country Park

① *Craigallian Rd, T0131-956 6100, www.mugdock-country-park.org.uk.*

Within easy reach of the city, north of the suburb of Milngavie (pronounced 'Mullguy'), is Mugdock Country Park, sitting between Glasgow and the Campsie Fells. It offers some fine walking along marked trails and includes the first section of the West Highland Way which starts in Milngavie. There are regular trains from Central station to Milngavie. You can either walk from here for three miles across Drumclog Moor or take the Mugdock bus from the station.

Paisley

West of Glasgow, close to the airport, is the town that gave its name to the famous fabric design copied from Kashmiri shawls. Paisley grew up around its 12th-century roots and by the 19th century was a major producer of printed cotton and woollen cloth, specializing in the production of the eponymous imitation shawls.

In the town centre, opposite the town hall, is **Paisley Abbey** ① *T0141-889 7654, www. paisleyabbey.org.uk, Mon-Sat 1000-1530, free*, founded in 1163 but destroyed during the Wars of Independence in the early 14th century. It was rebuilt soon after, but fell into ruin from the 16th century. Successive renovations took place, ending with a major restoration in the 1920s. The façade doesn't do justice to the wonderfully spacious interior, which includes exceptional stained-glass windows and an impressive choir. Also of note is the 10th-century Barochan Cross, at the eastern end of the north nave. The 46-m-high tower is occasionally made open to the public. There's also a gift shop and tea room.

In the High Street is the **Paisley Museum and Art Gallery** ① *T0141-889 3151, Tue-Sat 1000-1700, Sun 1400-1700, free*, with a huge collection of the world famous Paisley shawls and an interesting display of the history of weaving. Also on the High Street is another imposing ecclesiastical monument, the **Thomas Coats Memorial Church** ① *T0141-889 9980, viewing by appointment*, built by the great Victorian thread maker and one of the grandest Baptist churches in Europe. **Coats Observatory** ① *Oakshaw St, T0141-889 2013, Tue-Sat 1100-1600, Sun 1400-1700, free, public telescope viewing Tue and Thu 1830-2100 Nov-Mar*, has some interesting displays on climate, seismology and astronomy. Another interesting sight is the **Sma' Shot Cottages** ① *George Pl, off New St, T0141-889 1708, www. smashot.co.uk, Wed and Sat 1200-1600 Apr-Sep*. These are fully restored and furnished 18th-century weavers' cottages, with photographs and various artefacts. There's also a tea room with home baking. To the south of Paisley is the **Gleniffer Braes Country Park**, which is a great place for a walk in the hills. To get there, take the B775 south of town. For Paisley's latest events and openings consult www.renfrewshire.gov.uk. There is a **tourist information centre** ① *9A Gilmour St, T0141-889 0711*.

Around Glasgow

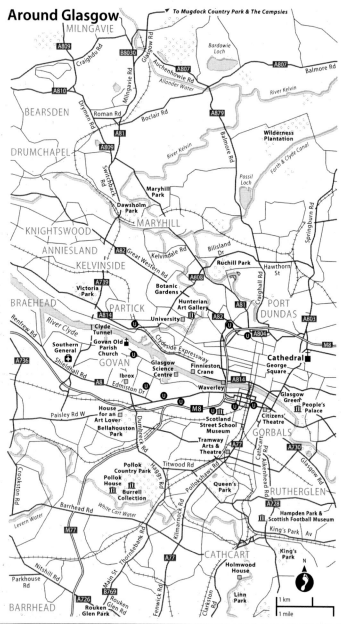

Firth of Clyde

West of Glasgow, the banks of the Clyde are still lined with the hulking ghosts of this great river's shipbuilding heritage. West of the Erskine Bridge, which connects the north and south banks of the Clyde, is **Port Glasgow**, the first of a series of grim towns, which sprawl along the southern coast of the Firth of Clyde. It was developed as the city's first harbour in the late 17th century, but there's little to detain visitors today. Just before Port Glasgow, however, west of Langbank, just off the M8/A8, is **Finlaystone Estate** ① T01475-540505, www.finlaystone.co.uk, gardens all year 1000-1700, tea room Apr-Sep 1100-1700, £4, concession £3, a Georgian mansion house set in sprawling landscaped grounds and featuring a walled garden, woodland play area, visitor centre and conservatory tea room. There are superb views across the Clyde.

About 30 miles west of Glasgow, **Greenock** was the first dock on the Clyde, back in the early 18th century and was the birthplace, in 1736, of James Watt, whose development of the steam engine contributed so much to the Industrial Revolution. Greenock today doesn't look particularly appealing, but it has its attractions. On the quay is the **Customs House**, a neoclassical building where Robert Burns and Adam Smith were once employees. While you're here, you should visit the **McLean Museum and Art Gallery** ① 15 Kelly St, near Greenock West station, T01475-715624, www.inverclyde.gov.uk/museums, Mon-Sat 1000-1700, free. The museum contains a collection of items belonging to the town's most famous son, James Watt, including a precursor to the photocopier which he patented around 1790 and was used in offices right up until the 1940s. There is also an Egyptology collection featuring items brought back from 19th-century explorations. A small gallery has works by the Glasgow Boys (see box, page 45) as well as by Fergusson, Cadell and Peploe.

Three miles west of Greenock is the shabby old seaside resort of **Gourock**. Gourock is the terminal for the ferry to Dunoon, on the Cowal Peninsula, see page 84. Eight miles south of Gourock is **Wemyss Bay**, departure point for ferries to Rothesay, on the Isle of Bute. Every summer this place used to be packed full of holidaying Glaswegians heading 'doon the watter' to Rothesay, and the magnificent Victorian train station is a proud legacy of those days. **CalMac** and **Argyll Ferries** timetables are available online with train connections from Glasgow.

The **Isle of Bute** is a relaxing place to visit, offering walks and one very beguiling attraction, Mount Stuart; see below. Vestiges of its Victorian holiday heyday can be glimpsed in the main town and port, **Rothesay**. Don't miss its stately bathrooms by the quayside. A small donation allows entrance to gaze upon the beautiful tiles, marble detailing and Adamant urinals. At the end of the town's Victorian Esplanade is the art-deco gem Rothesay Pavilion, a hub of community life set for long-overdue restoration.

Mount Stuart

① Rothesay, T01700-503 877, www.mountstuart.com, open late Mar to 31 Oct, gardens 1000-1800, house 1100-1700, gardens £6.50, house and gardens £11.

The ancestral home of the marquesses of Bute is an imposing Victorian Gothic revival pile that dates back to the time of Queen Anne. Set aside at least four hours to view the palace and explore its 120 ha of woodland, lawn and blossom-heavy shrubbery. The theatrical interiors are best viewed with one of the eccentric guides who supply some tasty historical detail.

John Patrick Crichton-Stuart (1847-1900), the third Marquess of Bute, and architect Sir Robert Rowand Anderson masterminded the present structure and opulently crafted interior. The third Marquess inherited a vast wealth from his mineral-mining father. But he did not keep his money to himself; this scholarly, religious man, with a passion for ancient history, Medievalism and the occult, was a notable philanthropist. This all becomes clear amid the intricately woven silk wall coverings, elaborate wood carvings, fantastic frescos, stunning stained glass and delicately fashioned marble.

Its present owner, the seventh Marquess of Bute, AKA Johnny Dumfries or Johnny Bute, accumulated a £12 million overdraft so had to take drastic action to get back into the black. The Marquess opened the house to the public and sold off some family silver, including a fancy German commode worth £5000. With its colonnaded hall festooned with the symbolism of astrology and astronomy, Carrara marble chapel, and baronial bedrooms, it's now a popular wedding venue; Stella McCartney – the fashion-designing daughter of Paul – tied the knot here. A modern visitor centre, garden shop and farm plus a summertime contemporary arts programme make Mount Stuart a beguiling day trip destination. There's a free shuttle ride for those not up to the walk between the visitor centre and house.

Dumbarton Castle
ⓘ T01389-732167, Apr-Sep daily 0930-1730, Oct-Mar Mon-Wed and Sat-Sun 0930-1630, £4.50, concession £2.70, get off at Dumbarton East station.

Once the capital of the ancient Britons of Strathclyde, Dumbarton dates back as far as the fifth century, when it was an important trading centre and of strategic importance. Today, though, it's a pretty awful place, and of little importance to tourists. It's best to avoid the town and head straight for the spectacular Dumbarton Castle, perched on top of Dumbarton Rock, which is surrounded by water on three sides and commands excellent views over the Clyde estuary. This has been a strategic fortress for 2000 years, though most of the current buildings date from the 18th century or later.

If you're interested in shipbuilding then you should visit the Scottish Maritime Museum's **Denny Ship Model Experiment Tank** ⓘ Castle St, T01389-763 444, www.scottishmaritimemuseum.org, Mon-Sat 1000-1600, £2, concession £1.50. This provides an atmospheric opportunity to immerse yourself in the world of the Victorian ship designer. The 1882 structure retains many original features including the famous 91-m-long test tank. The main site of the Scottish Maritime Museum is on the Ayrshire coast at Irvine.

The Clyde Valley
The River Clyde undergoes a series of changes as it begins the journey from its source, 80 miles southeast of Glasgow, through the orchards and market gardens of pretty Clydesdale and the abandoned coal mines of North Lanarkshire on its way to the former shipyards of Glasgow. The M74 motorway follows the course of the river, straddled by the valley's two largest towns, Hamilton and Motherwell. Sandwiched between them is Strathclyde Country Park, a huge recreational area featuring a 81-ha man-made loch popular with watersports enthusiasts. The M74 then turns south towards the border with England, while the A72 takes up the task of shadowing the river to Lanark, the most interesting focus of this area, standing as it does beside the fascinating village of New Lanark

The town of **Blantyre**, now more of a suburb of Hamilton, is famous as the birthplace of David Livingstone (1813-1873), the notable Victorian missionary and explorer, who felt the white man's burden more than most and took off to Africa in 1840 to bring Christianity to the natives. He was born in the humble surroundings of a one-roomed tenement, and worked in the local cotton mill before educating himself and taking a medical degree. The entire tenement block has been transformed into the **David Livingstone Centre** ⓘ 165 Station Rd, T0844-493 2207, www.nts.org.uk, Mar-Dec Mon-Sat 1000-1700, Sun 1230-1700,

£6.50, child/concession £5, which tells the story of his life, including his battle against slave traders and that famous meeting with Stanley. There's also an African-themed café, gift shop and garden. The centre is a short walk from the train station.

A 30-minute walk down the river towards Uddingston brings you to the substantial red sandstone ruin of **Bothwell Castle** ① *T01698-816894, Apr-Sep Mon-Sun 0930-1730, Oct daily 0930-1630, Nov-Mar Mon-Wed and Sat-Sun 0930-1630, £4, children £2.40*. This is commonly regarded as the finest 13th-century stronghold in the country and was fought over repeatedly by the Scots and English during the Wars of Independence. It has withstood the ravages of time well and is still hugely impressive.

Southwest of Blantyre is the **National Museum of Scottish Country Life** ① *Philipshill Rd, Wester Kittochside, East Kilbride, T0300-123 6789, www.nms.ac.uk, daily 1000-1700, £6.50, concession £5.50, children free*, which gives an insight into the lives of people in rural Scotland. Situated on a 70-ha site complete with Georgian farmhouse, the land was gifted by the Reid family who farmed here for 400 years. The Reids resisted intensive farming methods, so the land is still rich in wild plants that have disappeared from much of the farming land in Britain. The Exhibition Building has galleries on the environment, rural technologies and people, and has thousands of exhibits, including the oldest threshing machine in the world, dating back to 1805. The Historic Farm is worked to demonstrate traditional agricultural methods of the 1950s, following the seasons to show ploughing, seeding time, haymaking and harvest. There is also an Events Area with demonstrations of the working collection, plus a shop and café. Various seasonal events are held here including Go Wild activities for kids, Classic Cars and Heavy Horse shows and a Country Fair.

Hamilton has the longest history of any in the area, with associations with Mary, Queen of Scots, Cromwell and the Covenanters, who were defeated by Monmouth at nearby Bothwell Bridge, in 1679. The town today is unremarkable but a mile or so south, at Ferniegair, are the gates to **Chatelherault** ① *T01698-426 213, www.visitlanarkshire.com, free, Main house Sun-Thu (check latest for Fri and Sat as may be closed for private functions)*, an extensive country park and impressive hunting lodge and summer house, built in 1732 by William Adam for the Dukes of Hamilton. There are ornamental gardens and 10 miles of trails to explore along the deep wooded glen of the Avon, past the 16th-century ruins of Cadzow Castle and into the surrounding countryside. The Ranger service offers guided walks around the park. Check the website for upcoming family-orienatated events.

Within the bounds of nearby Strathclyde Park is the **Hamilton Mausoleum** ① *129 Muir St, www.visitlanarkshire.com, Mon-Sat 1000-1700, Sun 1200-1700, £2, children £1*, a huge burial vault of the Hamilton family. It's an eerie place with the longest lasting echo for an building in the world, allegedly, allegedly, allegedly…

The little market town of **Lanark**, 25 miles southeast of Glasgow, sits high above the River Clyde. Most people come here to visit the immaculately restored village of **New Lanark** ① *T01555-661345, www.newlanark.org, visitor centre Apr-Oct 1000-1700, Nov-Mar 1000-1600, access to the village at all times, one ticket to all attractions: £8.50, concession/ children £7*. To get there take a train from Glasgow Central to Lanark then 1.5 miles/2.5 km bus/taxi to site. It's one of the region's most fascinating sights, a mile below the town of Lanark, beside the river Clyde. In 1785 David Dale and Richard Arkwright founded the community around a cotton-spinning centre, but it was Dale's son-in-law, Robert Owen, who took over the management in 1798 and who pioneered the revolutionary social experiment. He believed in a more humane form of capitalism and believed the welfare of his workers to be crucial to industrial success. He provided them with decent housing, a co-operative store (the forerunner of the modern co-operative movement), adult educational facilities, the world's first day nursery and the social centre of the community, the modestly titled Institute for the Formation of Character. Here, in the visitor centre, you can see an introductory video about New Lanark and its founders, see original textile machinery and join the atmospheric Annie McLeod Experience Ride, which tells the story of a girl at New Lanark in 1820. Audio-visual technology allows you to see the 'ghost' of Annie McLeod (an imaginary mill girl) on stage, telling you the story of life in 19th-century New Lanark. Other interesting displays and interactive galleries bring life in the mills alive. There is also a reconstruction of an early classroom. You can wander through the village and see the 1920s shop, a restored mill-worker's house and even Robert Owen's House. There's also a tea room and gift shop. Don't miss the fabulous roof garden with contemporary landscaped terrain and wonderful views. There's a **tourist information centre** ① *Lanark Horsemarket, 90 m west of the train station, T0141-661 661, open year round*, who can book accommodation. It takes about 45 minutes to get here from the city and there's plenty to keep you occupied for the day if combined with a walk in the wooded Falls of Clyde Nature Reserve, just beyond the village. You can visit the **Scottish Wildlife Trust (SWT) Centre** ① *T0141-665 262, daily 1100-1700 (1200-1600 Jan-Feb), £2, concessions £1*, housed in the old dyeworks, which provides information about the history and wildlife of the area. Activities include guided walks spotting badgers and bats, honeybee observation and getting up close to peregrine falcons.

Within walking distance of the village are the stunning **Corra Linn waterfalls** – the total distance, including the extension, is 5.5 miles. Allow three to four hours there and back, and wear boots or strong shoes as some parts can be muddy. Starting from the village, walk past the SWT centre and up the stone steps into the nature reserve above Dundaff Linn, the smallest of the three waterfalls on the walk. A riverside boardwalk takes you past a 200-year-old weir, and just beyond the end of the boardwalk go right at a junction to pass Bonnington power station. Steps then lead up to a viewing platform above the dramatic Corra Linn, the highest falls on the Clyde, where the river plunges 27 m in three stages. Continue up the steps and follow the path through woodlands to reach another set of falls at Bonnington Linn. You can retrace your steps back to the village, or extend the walk by crossing the weir at Bonnington Linn and turning right down the track on the opposite bank, taking a narrow path on the right after a few hundred yards. Take care here as the path is very close to the lip of the gorge. After about a mile, the path leads you to the crumbling ruin of Corra Castle. To return to Bonnington Linn, retrace your steps for about 100 yards and then follow the vehicle track on the right.

Five miles northwest of Lanark is the village of **Crossford**, from where you can visit **Craignethan Castle** ① *Apr-Sep daily 0930-1730, Sun 1400-1630, £4, concessions £2.40*, an ornate tower house standing over the River Nethan. It was built by Sir James Hamilton for James V, in 1530, and was last major castle to be built in Scotland. Mary, Queen of Scots left from here to do battle at Langside (at Queen's Park in Glasgow), where she was defeated and fled to France before her eventual imprisonment. The castle, like so many others in Scotland, is said to be haunted by her ghost. To get there take a bus from Lanark to Crossford, then it's a 15-minute walk.

Glasgow listings

For hotel and restaurant price codes and other relevant information, see pages 9-11.

⊖ Where to stay

City centre, Buchanan St and Sauciehall St *p24, p34 and p37, map p26*

££££ Crowne Plaza, Congress Rd, T0871-423 4942, www.ihg.com. Massive mirrored-glass structure with nearly 300 rooms next to the SECC and 'Armadillo' on the banks of the Clyde. It's a bit out of the city centre but has good views of the river and is conveniently situated opposite the glittering Science Centre too. Facilities include restaurants and leisure centre with pool. Highlight of a stay is often the panoramic lift. Might be a tad impersonal and corporate for some tastes.

£££ Baby Abode, 129 Bath St, T0141-221 6789, www.abodehotels.co.uk. Housed in an elegant Edwardian building on Bath Street with many original architectural features including a wonderful old gated lift running through the central atrium. Neutral colours and mainstream contemporary design go with the historic handsome features including wood panelling in their high-ceilinged 'Fabulous' rooms. Excellent cooked breakfasts– for an extra £10 per head – are served in the smart lounge.

£££ Carlton George Hotel, 44 West George St, T0141-3536373, www.carlton hotels.co.uk. Established chain with 65 rooms and Glasgow's 1st rooftop restaurant. A traditional, plush hotel very close to George Sq and the shops. Rooms include complimentary minibar, Wi-Fi and SKY TV package. Some may find it all a little staid, dated and uninspiring. Discounted parking at nearby Buchanan St.

£££ Hilton, 1 William St, T0141-204 5555, www.hilton.co.uk. Gigantic, futuristic-looking luxury hotel with 319 rooms. Expect some good facilities, including a leisure centre and shopping mall. The Executive Floor still delivers but many of the standard rooms look a little tired.

£££ Indigo, 75 Waterloo St, T0871-423 4917, www.ihg.com. A stylish conversion of an impressive Victorian building, by the Inter Continental Hotel group. Public areas including the large **Limelight Bar & Grill**, which has pale walls with wooden floors and lots of bright coloured furnishings. Spacious guest rooms have oversized beds with wool rugs and excellent facilities including complimentary minibar, free Wi-Fi, flatscreen TV and iPod docking station. The stylish bathrooms have large rain-head showers. Lots of room options to choose from.

£££ Malmaison, 278 West George St, T0141-572 1000, www.malmaison.com. A converted episcopal church with a striking lobby and 72 rooms by an established designer chain that can now be found in many UK cities. Stylish urban accommodation, perfect for 30-somethings taking a short break, although it has lost some of its lustre. The chic rooms have plasma screens and music systems, while the hotel's dark wood-filled brasserie attracts plenty of diners. It's a handy location for nightlife and shopping.

£££ Radisson SAS, 301 Argyle St, T0141-204 3333, www.radisson.com/glasgowuk. Shiny glass branch of this reliable chain near Central Station. Cavernous lobby area has a bar which is a bit of a social hub. Among the 247 rooms the standard ones are a bit dull while corner suites offer something special. It's handily placed for the shops and other city centre sights and also has a health club with a 20-m swimming pool.

££ Adelaide's, 209 Bath St, T0141-248 4970, www.adelaides.co.uk. A handsome 'Greek' Thomson restoration, with 8 simply furnished rooms in the heart of the city centre. This place offers the chance to stay somewhere a bit different at a reasonable price. Good budget option, especially for lovers of architecture in Glasgow for over 3 nights (check online deals for 3 nights or more). Various size rooms including 2 family-friendly options. .

££ Babbity Bowster, 16-18 Blackfriars St, T0141-552 5055, www.babbitybowster.com. A local institution and one of the first of the Merchant City townhouses to be renovated. Typical Glaswegian hospitality, a near-legendary pub and an excellent restaurant. The 6 simple en suite rooms on the second floor. For the curious: Babbity Bowster is an old Scottish country dance.

££ Brunswick Hotel, 106-108 Brunswick St, T0141-552 0001, www.brunswickhotel.co.uk. Small minimalist-style hotel with 21 rooms in the heart of the Merchant City – handy for those seeking nightlife on the doorstep. Bargain rates can be had but a word of warning: this place can get noisy at night. Their excellent bar-restaurant, **Brutti ma Buoni** (that's 'ugly but good' in Italian), is probably the best thing about it.

££ CitizenM, 60 Renfrew St, T01782-488 3490, www.citizenm.com. Futuristic Dutch chain contemporary hotel mixing truly stylish interiors, efficient automated services and a hip international atmosphere near Glasgow's nightlife. An open-plan area allows self-service check with friendly help at hand. Guests mingle, eat and drink in **CanteenM** till 0200, play on computers and in lounges relax with art books and Vitra design classics, including iconic Eames and Panton chairs. Guest rooms are compact pods with XL king-size beds, mood lighting, power shower and remote-control gadgetry. It's an affordable boutique-hotel experience, not for technophobes or those who don't like to share space (no twins – just doubles).

££ Millennium Hotel, George Sq, T0141-332 6711, www.millennium-hotels.com. Huge 18th-century hotel in the heart of the city, right next to Queen St station with 117 rooms. It's an ideal location for those wanting to explore both the Merchant City and the shops in Buchanan St, while the conservatory bar on the ground floor provides great people-watching potential. Due a refurb at the time of writing.

££ Rab Ha's, 83 Hutcheson St, T0141-572 0400, www.rabhas.com. There are just 4 good-value rooms available at this central Merchant City institution best known for its food. Stylish decor with light, bright contemporary rooms, crisp sheets and white bathrobes. There's free Wi-Fi and flatscreen TV with Sky. It's above the pub so expect some nightly noise and high spirits. Rab Ha, in case you're wondering, was a famous Glasgow glutton.

£ Rennie Mackintosh Art School Hotel, 218-220 Renfrew St, T0141-333 9992, www.renniemackintoshhotels.com. A small hotel offering friendly service and superb value for money in a handy central location. It's 24 en suite rooms have free Wi-Fi and tea/coffee making facilities. Discounted car parking at **ThistleCar Park**. No lift.

£ The Victorian House Hotel, 212 Renfrew St, T0141-332 0129, www.thevictorian.co.uk. This place is all about price but you get a handy near the art college, Tenement House and nightlife. 60 functional rooms of various sizes (some suitable for families and groups), free Wi-Fi, tea- and coffee-making facilities and Scottish breakfast included. Consistently delivers good value for those on a tight budget.

Self-catering and serviced accommodation

A good place to start research into apartments is www.citybaseapartments.com, T0845-226 9831, a broker for many properties in Glasgow.

Max Serviced Apartments, 38 Bath St, T0844-557 5130/0844-557 5134, www.max-servicedapartments.co.uk. Smart contemporary apartments in a handsome Victorian building with nightlife and restaurant action on the doorstep. Opened in 2012 is Max's other Glasgow property **Olympic House** – on George Sq – with 45 1- to 2-bedroom apartments. Both locations cost £80 per night for a twin/double.

The Serviced Apartment Company, SACO House, 53 Cochrane St, T0845-122 0405, www.sacoapartments.co.uk. A well-established nationwide rental company that manages 3 apartment buildings in the Merchant City and one in the West End. From £66 per night, with a minimum stay of 2 or 3 nights.

The Spires, 77 Glassford St, T0845-270 0090/01224-201040, www.thespires.co.uk. This company manages a range of apartments in Merchant City. From small bedroom suites to 3-room penthouse apartments sleeping 6 people. Nightly rates £145-475.

Tolbooth Apartments, 24 High St, www.principalapartments.com. Range of modern 1- and 2-bed apartments in a good spot to access Glasgow's prime shopping streets, the Merchant City, the Barras and Barrowland and the artsy hangouts on Trongate/King St.

Hostels
£ Euro Hostel, 318 Clyde St, T0141-222 2828, www.euro-hostels.com. 364 beds, all rooms with en suite facilities, includes continental breakfast. A huge multi-storey building overlooking the Clyde. A private room for 2 starts at £32.

Campus accommodation
University of Strathclyde, T0141-548 3503, www.rescat.strath.ac.uk. Also has a wide range of B&B lodgings available in its various halls of residence across the city, mostly Jun-Sep, though a few are open all year round. The Campus Village on the John Anderson Campus in the heart of Glasgow is the University of Strathclyde's largest single site for accommodation. It's centrally located amid landscaped gardens, just 5 mins' walk from George Sq and Queen St Railway Station. There are around 500 single rooms available from £28. An en suite room costs £40. Breakfast is available. Self-catering flats can be rented with a 3-night minimum stay. For 4-6 people: prices start at £212-313 for 3 nights. Visitors get the use of the student facilities including restaurant, bars, laundrette and sports centres.

Camping
£ Craigendmuir Park Campsie View, Stepps, 4 miles northeast of the centre just off the A80 and a 15-min walk from Stepps station, T0141-779 4159, www.craigendmuir.co.uk. It's a spacious campsite that caters for caravans, motor homes and tents. There are chalets and static homes as well. Prices start at £20 for a 2-man tent. Facilities include shower block, laundrette and shop.

East End *p31, map p26*
££ Cathedral House, 28/32 Cathedral Sq, T0141-552 3519, www.cathedralhouse hotel.com. A wonderfully atmospheric small hotel set in a red-sandstone Victorian Gothic revival mansion with turrets overlooking the cathedral and Necropolis. There are 7 rooms including one that is said to be haunted. Their little bar and summertime restaurant menu both get mixed reviews, especially in the winter months.

West End and along the Clyde *p39 and p46, maps p40 and p42*
££££ Hotel du Vin, 1 Devonshire Gardens, T0141-339 2001, www.hotelduvin.com. A luxury bolt hole with 49 rooms and suites. This chain hotel is still doing that contemporary take on an exclusive Scottish members' club, with new tartan patterns, flock wallpaper, mountains of cushions, carefully chosen artworks and antiques, and attentive service. It also has an elegant bistro. It's hosted many a celebrity including Tina Turner and George Clooney but is perhaps less fashionable of late.

££ Argyll Hotel, 973 Sauchiehall St, T0141-337 3313, www.argyllhotelglasgow. co.uk. A traditional hotel in a refurbished Georgian building, with 38 functional rooms and an adjoining **Argyll Guest House** offering 20 cheaper rooms, from £60. It's located opposite Kelvingrove and is handy for the West End attractions. The Riverside Museum is a short walk away so all-in-all it's a good-value option for families especially. There's a bar/restaurant, **Sutherlands**, with fireplace serving Scots fare. It's somewhat of a cultural centre running on-site events including a Murder Mystery Evening, Whisky Tasting and Ceildh nights – as well as walking tours. The smarter hotel rooms have free Wi-Fi, TV and tea- and coffee-making facilities.

££ Hilton Glasgow Grosvenor, 1-10 Grosvenor Terr, Great Western Rd, T0141-339 8811, www.hilton.co.uk. A smaller, 4-star, version of the city centre hotel (see above) situated in a traditional West End terrace. This is a good choice for nature lovers as about half their rooms have views of the Botanic Gardens opposite. Avoid the other rooms overlooking a car park.

££ Kelvin Hotel, 15 Buckingham Terr, Great Western Rd, T0141-339 7143, www.kelvinhotel.com. A family-run hotel in an impressive West End Victorian grade 'A' listed terrace near Byres Rd and Botanic Gardens. 21 high-ceilinged guest rooms with TV and free Wi-Fi. The kitchen facilities are available to residents. For longer stays and families ask about their **Kelvin** apartment.

££ Kirklee Hotel, 11 Kensington Gate, T0141-334 5555, www.kirkleehotel.co.uk. A long-established B&B in a beautiful Edwardian town house with a tranquil garden. Public rooms have an eyeful of tartan carpet, handsome dark wood panelling and original fireplaces. The 9 well-maintained en suite rooms have free Wi-Fi, TV and tea- and coffee-making facilities. Close to bars and restaurants on Byres Rd and the Botanic Gardens.

££ Manor Park Hotel, 28 Balshagray Dr, T0141-339 2143, www.themanorpark.com. This West End guesthouse in a homely Victorian building is a Glasgow oddity in that Gaelic is spoken and actively promoted. Well-kept rooms with Wi-Fi, tea- and coffee-making facilities and TV. It's a stimulating choice for anyone seeking a rich taste of Scottish Gaelic culture.

££ Sandyford Hotel, 904 Sauchiehall St, T0141-334 0000, www.sandyfordhotel glasgow.com. Good value B&B convenient for the West End and Clydeside attractions including the SECC and Kelvingrove. 55 simply furnished modern rooms with free Wi-Fi internet access. Popular with groups and stag/hen parties at weekends so expect some rolling noise at night. Weekdays are more civilized.

£ Heritage Hotel, 1 Alfred Terr, 625 Great Western Rd, T0141-339 6955, www.the heritagehotel.net. Exceptional value B&B in 2 adjoining Victorian town houses close to the West End action. 27 plain, functional rooms in various sizes that can accommodate up to 4 people.

Hostels

£ Bunkum Backpackers, 26 Hillhead St, T0141-581 4481, www.bunkumglasgow.co.uk. A basic, cheap 36-bed hostel in a Victorian town house, with kitchen facilities. No night time curfew. Free Wi-fi. From £16 for a twin.

£ SYHA Youth Hostel, 7/8 Park Terr, T0141-332 3004, www.syha.org.uk. 135 beds. This great 4-star hostel is a cut above Glasgow's largely awful hostels. All rooms have en suite facilities and there are lots of room options. Catering is available including packed lunches and dinners. Continental breakfast is £4.50 extra; cooked breakfast is £6. It gets very busy in Jul/Aug so you'll need to book ahead. Open 24 hrs. It's a 10-min walk from Kelvinbridge Underground station, or take a bus from Central station and get off at the first stop on Woodlands Rd, then head up the first turning left (Lynedoch St). An ideal choice for families and groups especially. Twin/double rooms start at £57; quadruples are £98; 6-bedded room £141; and 8-person self-catering flat with 2 bathrooms at £188.

Self-catering and serviced accommodation

City Apartments, 401 North Woodside Rd, T0141-342 4060, www.glasgowhotelsand apartments.co.uk. Next to the **Albion Hotel**, close to Kelvinbridge Underground and handy for the park and West End attractions. 4 studio apartments with kitchen and free

Wi-Fi access. From £60 for a single and £75 for a twin/double.

Dreamhouse Inc, T0141-332 3620, www.dreamhouseapartments.com. Have several luxury serviced apartments in Lynedoch Cres. Nightly rates range from £120 to £215.

Embassy Apartments, 8 Kelvin Dr, T0141-946 6698, www.glasgowhotels andapartments.co.uk. 6 apartments of various sizes in a converted Victorian terraced house in the West End, about a mile from the city centre. All are en suite with free Wi-Fi, TV and ironing facilities. Good for groups as large apartments sleep up to 5 people. From £75 for a twin/double.

White House, 12 Cleveden Cres, T0141-339 9375, www.whitehouse-apartments.com. Lots of options available from the long-established company based near the Great Western Rd in the leafy West End. There are 32 apartments in the main location and others spread around – of varying sizes and quality (studio flats to 4-bedrooms). A twin/double apartment starts at £75 or £444 per week.

Campus accommodation

University of Glasgow, contact the Conference and Visitor Services, 3 The Sq, T0141-330 5385, www.gla.ac.uk/services/cvso/accommodation/universityofglasgow residences. There is a range of self-catering accommodation, available Jun-Sep, within 4 campus complexes: **Queen Margaret Residences**, **Cairncross House**, **Wolfson Hall**, **Murano Street Village** and **Kelvinhaugh Gate**. Prices range from £22 for basic single in a self-catering apartment to £70 for a twin. Contact the Conference and Visitor Services office for the latest deals and availability.

South Side p49

£££ Mar Hall, Earl of Mar Estate, Refrew. T0141-812 9999, www.marhall.com. Sprawling Victorian mansion built in the 1840s now a spa/golf resort a short drive form Glasgow Airport. 53 rooms, many in palatial style, with calming decor, rich fabrics and smart bathrooms. Afternoon tea is served in the long, atmospheric Grand Hall. There are lots of facilities including 2 restaurants, bar, Earl of Mar golf course on the doorstep, pool and Aveda Spa treatments and gym.

£££ Sherbrooke Castle Hotel, 11 Sherbrooke Av, T0141-427 4227, www.sherbrooke.co.uk. Beguiling hotel housed in a Victorian Gothic pile with baronial turrets near Pollok Park. Tartan and period furnishings abound. Guest rooms have been recently refurbished and have contemporary bathrooms, free Wi-Fi, hospitality tray and decent TVs. There's a spacious suite with a lounge high up in the main tower. It's a good base for exploring the attractions of the south side as it's only about a mile from the Burrell collection.

££ Glasgow Guest House, 56 Dumbrek Rd, T0141-427 0219, www.glasgow-guest-house.co.uk. Excellent value choice near Pollok Park. Smart accommodation in an informal semi-detached house setting. Self-contained apartments are available which are ideal for groups and families. Cooked B&B-style breakfast included, which is served in the relaxing conservatory or garden.

Around Glasgow p53

There are plenty of B&Bs in the Clyde Coast and a handful in Lanark and New Lanark. Here's a selection of standout places and most interesting places to stay.

Firth of Clyde

££ Munro's B&B, Ardmory Rd, T01700-502 346, www.visitmunros.co.uk. A homely B&B on a hill above Rothesay set in beautiful gardens with a pond and views run by helpful English hosts. The 6 en suite rooms in relaxing hues of various sizes are suited to couples, groups and families. A ground-floor room has access for disabled guests. They run a bread-making school here. The excellent breakfasts are included in the tariff.

New Lanark

£££ New Lanark Mill Hotel, T01555-667200, newlanarkhotel.co.uk. Converted mill with superb views over the mighty Clyde waters and countryside around the New Lanark heritage site. Among the 38 simply furnished, well-maintained en suite rooms and 8 converted self-catering Waterhouses are plenty of options for couples, groups, families and the disabled. Superb facilities include heated swimming pool, restaurant, bar, lounge and gym.

£ New Lanark Youth Hostel, Wee Row, Rosedale St, New Lanark, T01555-666710, www.syha.org.uk. Beautifully situated in Wee Row by the river within easy strike of the heritage site and Clyde Falls Wildlife Reserve. Great for single travellers, couples, groups and families on a budget. 60 beds from £17 a night with small en suite rooms also available. Twins £40, triples £70, quads £90, 5-bedded £112 and 6-bedded from £135.

❷ Restaurants

City centre, Buchanan St and Sauciehall St p24, p34 and p37, map p26

£££ Amber Regent, 50 West Regent St, T0141-3311655. www.amberregent.com. Long-established Chinese restaurant housed in stately formal dining rooms. Those on a tight budget can also indulge themselves, with half-price main courses before 1900 Wed-Fri and all night Sun-Tue. A well-respected Glasgow eatery that can get very busy, so it's best to book ahead.

£££ Brian Maule at Chardon d'Or, 176 West Regent St, T0141-248 3801, www.brianmaule.com. Closed Sun. Opulent venue catering very much to well lunched businessmen. Head chef was trained at the Roux brothers' Michel-starred **Le Gavroche** in London so expect French-influenced fare using quality Scots produce. Pre-theatre and lunch deals are worth considering. Cookery demos staged here.

£££ Gamba, 225a West George St, T0141-572 0899, www.gamba.co.uk. Closed Sun. A popular fish restaurant famed for the freshest fish cooked with flair and imagination. Expect seasonal dishes including the springtime favourite: roast hake, red pepper, garlic oil, tiger prawns, sweet soy and fragrant rice. A member of the **Sustainable Restaurant Association** (SRA). The decor is stylish with a few nods to the marine world. A great choice for a special occasion. Try their legendary fish soup to start.

£££ Ho Wong, 82 York St, T0141-221 3550, www.ho-wong.com. Closed Sun lunch. Tucked away just off Argyle St, this Chinese restaurant doesn't look much from the outside but inside awaits a memorable Cantonese culinary experience and the city's finest Szechuan food. It's not cheap though.

£££ Rogano's, 11 Exchange Pl, T0141-248 4055, www.roganoglasgow.com. A Glasgow culinary institution. Designed in the style of the Cunard liner, *Queen Mary*, and built by the same workers. Looks like the set of a Hollywood blockbuster and you'll need a similar budget to pay the bill, but the seafood is truly sensational. **Café Rogano** offers a less stylish alternative, but it's a lot easier on the pocket.

££ Arta, housed in the Old Cheesemarket, 13-19 Walls St, T0141-552 2101, www.arta.co.uk. Thu-Sat 1700-late only. A stylish Spanish restaurant that serves tapas, tortillas and meaty stews. Housed in the swanky **Corinthian Club** (see below) within the Old Cheesemarket, the decor is faux-Spanish with mosaics and huge candelabras. Bar open later.

££ Baby Grand, 3-7 Elmbank Gardens, T0141-248 4942, www.babygrandglasgow.com. Closed Sun from 1200. Chic jazz-café offering good bistro-style food when most other places have shut up shop. Enjoy late-night drinks and food and soothing jazz piano. They also do decent breakfasts. Pre-theatre and lunch menu deals.

££ Café Cossachock, 10 King St, T0141-553 0733, www.cossachok.com. Closed Sun lunch. Cosy, authentic-feeling Russian restaurant with a relaxed, informal atmosphere. Try a bowl of crimson borscht (beetroot and cabbage soup) – great on a damp Glasgow day, or a blini (pancake) stuffed with meat, spinach or even ice cream. The **Trongate** arts hub upstairs features galleries and studios worth visiting. It's also near the **Tron Theatre** and has an excellent for pre-theatre menu. More than just a good meal, a visit here provides an entire cultural experience.

££ Café Gandolfi, 64 Albion St, T0141-552 6813, www.cafegandolfi.com. Open daily 0800-late. The first of Glasgow's style bistro/brasseries opened back in 1979, and is housed in the handsome tiled offices of the old cheese market. The place is a venerable antique by today's contemporary design standards. Still comfortably continental, relaxed and soothing – take a pew at one of the beautiful sculptural tables all made by GSA graduate and furniture maker Tim Stead. Consult the daily specials, which may include grilled sea bass, pan-fried salmon or smoked venison. A reliable place for a snack or a leisurely late breakfast – they have a large choice from eggs Benedict to full Scottish.

££ City Merchant, 97-99 Candleriggs, T0141-553 1577, www.citymerchant.co.uk. Closed Sun lunch. The best of Scottish meat and game but it's the fish and seafood, which shine here. Perennial favourites include Cumbrae oysters, West Coast mussels, Hebridean salmon and grilled Dover sole. Carnivores get a look in too with Quality Meat Scotland approved Scots beef steaks. There are always a few imaginative veggie options too. Check out the excellent value 2- and 3-course set menus (available 1200-1830).

££ The Corinthian Club, 191 Ingram St, T0141-5521101, www.thecorinthianclub.co.uk. Open daily. There's a sense of occasion about going to the popular Corinthian

housed in tobacco merchant George Buchanan's former mansion. There are several bars, a nightclub, casino, private club and restaurant under an 8-m-high glass dome. Expect traditional dishes using the best Scots produce: salmon, beef, venison and shellfish galore. For best value check out the £15 2-course Market Menu served Sun-Wed. It's also a popular venue for afternoon tea. Reservations essential.

££ The Dhabba, 44 Candelriggs, T0141-553 1249, www.thedhabba.com. Open daily, Sat-Sun from 1300. Stylish Indian restaurant with contemporary dining rooms featuring lots of polished wood and gleaming cutlery. It's all about authentic Northern Indian cuisine here: Dhabba means 'diner' in Punjabi and the place specializes in Dum Pukht cuisine, where freshest ingredients are sealed so that they cook in their own juices. There's a wealth of vegetarian options available.

££ Esca, 27 Chisholm St, T0141-553 0880, www.esca-restaurant.co.uk. Open daily. A sleek, contemporary Italian restaurant with a friendly, relaxed atmosphere, serving classics with a twist here and there. Standard antipasti and primi pasta dishes – minestrone, bruschetta, carbonara and amaticana – share the menu with steaks and fish of the day. Set lunch menus and pre-theatre menu provide superb value and are well worth considering.

££ Fratelli Sarti, 121 Bath St, T0141-204 0440, www.fratelli-sarti.co.uk. Open daily. Everything you'd expect from a great Italian restaurant, and a lot more besides. **Sarti** is a real Glasgow institution, practically everyone in the city must have eaten here at some time. Good value food in authentic Italian surroundings – lots of chatter and bustle. Excellent pizza and the staff are great with kids. No wonder it's always busy – but be warned, service can be slow. Sister restaurants are at Renfield St and Wellington St.

££ The Green Room, Glasgow Royal Concert Hall (see page 76), 2 Sauchiehall St, T0141-353 8000. Open performance days only 1700-2130. Much more than a good place to eat before the show. **The Green Room** is a superb restaurant in its own right where you can indulge in the finest of Scottish produce. Good vegetarian selection.

££ Metropolitan, Merchant Sq, T0141-552 9402, www.metropolitan-bar.com. Open daily. Housed in the huge covered courtyard of the city's old Fruitmarket, this is a stylish, but slightly self-consciously bling, restaurant and bar with leather sofas, intimate booths and a dressed-up clientele. You can drink outside in the covered courtyard. Decent selection of seasonal meats (guinea fowl, venison and Angus steak) and seafood (rainbow trout, king prawns and clams) with contemporary garnishes and sides. The cocktail bar, piano lounge and champagne bar make this a glitzy venue for a special occasion. Pre-theatre (1700-1900; Mon-Tue till 2200) and set menus are worth considering.

££ Mussel Inn, 157 Hope St, T0843-289 2283, www.mussel-inn.com. Sun dinner only. Whitewashed contemporary space that serves superb value West Coast seafood – mussels, salmon, oysters, crab, haddock, prawns, scallops etc. Aberdeen Angus burgers and homemade desserts are served too. Expect the freshest ingredients and imaginative creations. Well worth a visit, especially for lunch and pre-theatre meal deals.

££ Schottische, 16-18 Blackfriars St, T0141-552 5055, www.babbitybowster.com/restaurant. Tue-Sat 1830-2300. Upstairs from the legendary **Babbity Bowsters** (see below). Excellent French/Scottish food at very affordable prices. Their cullen skink soup is a hearty starter. Expect seasonal produce; you might find venison as well as haggis on the menu, so if you've never tried it, here's your chance. Leave room for their diet-busting puddings – check the blackboard.

££ Tron Theatre, Chisholm St, T0141-552 8587, www.tron.co.uk/food-drink. Daily, Sun-Mon till 1800. Long-established restaurant offering a dining experience among the theatre set. Largely traditional hearty dishes

such as battered lemon sole and savoury pies, plus some imaginative sauces and veggie creations. Faint applause for the less than generous portions. The stylish bar is perfect for that pre-prandial tipple.

£ Babbity Bowster, see Where to stay, above. Open daily. You can't get away from this place, and why would you want to? Buzzing café-bar housed in a magnificent 18th-century building in the heart of the Merchant City. Traditional Scottish and French dishes served with flair. The bar is one of the city's perennial favourites.

£ Glasgow Noodle Bar, 482 Sauchiehall St, T0141-333 1883. Daily 1200-0500. Oriental fast food eaten from disposable containers with plastic chopsticks or forks. Very cheap chow and a reliable choice after a heavy night on the town.

£ Ichiban Japanese Noodle Café, 50 Queen St, T0141-204 4200. Daily 1200-2200. Excellent value, healthy Japanese specialities in sleek, modern surroundings.

£ Mono, Kings Court, King St, T0141-553 2400, www.monocafebar.com. Daily 1200-2200. Clean and simple, this contemporary vegan restaurant – part of the wonderful Monorail record shop/venue – is now an established favourite on Glasgow culinary scene. Expect a changing menu with dishes such as heaped tasty salads, Seitan burgers, Malaysian-style fried rice and smoked tofu wantons with spicy apricot conserve, and delicate Thai curry. All the beers and wines are vegan, the bread is organic, the coffee is ethical… so you can sip and munch with a sparkling clear conscience. Check the website for upcoming gigs here. Meal deals on a Mon.

£ Saramago Café Bar, at the CCA, 350 Sauchiehall St, T0141-332 7959. Mon-Sat 1000-2400. Set in the light-filled atrium and outdoor terrace of the **Centre for Contemporary Arts**, this café/restaurant serves contemporary Scottish fare. Home-baked breads and cakes, plus a well-thought-out selection of quality beers, wines and juices. The menu is flexible and varied so you can just drop in for a coffee and a snack.

There's a good choice from small tapas-style plates and salads to stonebaked pizzas and haggis fritters. Pre-theatre and lunch specials are available.

£ Stereo, 28 Renfield La, T0141-222 2254, www.stereocafebar.com. Food served daily 1100-2100. Housed within the music and comedy venue near Central Station, this welcoming vegan eatery has a sprawling set-list of platters, home-baked breads, tapas, soups, pizzas and daily specials. For an encore check the blackboard for daily homemade cakes and other sweet treats.

£ Trattoria Gia, 17 King St, T0141-552 7411, www.trattoriagia.weebly.com. Closed Mon. Very good value family-run Italian trattoria with a rustic decor near the Merchant City. Favourites include: spinach and ricotta tortellini with ragu, and chicken breast wrapped in parma ham and stuffed with mozzarella. The service is friendly and generally efficient.

£ Wee Curry Shop, 7 Buccleuch St, T0141-353 0777, www.weecurryshopglasgow.co.uk. Closed Sun lunch. Small in every sense – except flavour and value. Quite simply the best cheap curry this side of the Hindu Kush. Cosy, relaxed atmosphere. Good vegetarian options. Branches in the West End at 41 Byres Rd and 29 Aston La.

Cafés

Café Cosmo, 12 Rose St, T0141-332 6535. Daily food served 1200-1700, bar open till 2100. Part of the **Glasgow Film Theatre** (see Entertainment, page 75) and definitely worth knowing about, even if you're not a movie buff. The small menu focuses on tapas, mezze, baked potatoes and vegetarian soups. It's a great cheap lunch venue, especially for vegetarians, and the bar is a good meeting place for chin-stroking debates.

Doocot Café and Bar, The Lighthouse, 11 Mitchell La, T0141-221 1821, www.the lighthouse.co.uk/venue/eat. Mon-Sat 1000-1630, Sun 1200-1630. There's a nod to 1950s modernism at this light-filled café on

the top of **The Lighthouse** (see page 34). Grab one of the classic Eames chairs and peruse the latest menu of soups, sandwiches and light meals before immersing yourself in the world of architecture.

Mono, see above. Open late. Vegan restaurant and café housed within a cultural venue.

Willow Tea Rooms, 217 Sauchiehall St, T0141-332 0521, www.willowtearooms. co.uk. Mon-Sat 0900-1700, Sun 1100-1700. A recreation of the original **Miss Cranston's Tearooms**, designed by Charles Rennie Mackintosh and filled with many of his original features. Most visitors come here for the interior design, but they also offer a good selection of reasonably priced teas, sandwiches, cakes and scones, as well as hot meals. There is a sister branch at 97 Buchanan St, T0141-204 5242, which is licensed.

Where the Monkey Sleeps, 182 West Regent St, T0141-226 3406, www.monkey sleeps.com. Mon-Sat 0700-1700, Sat 1000-1900. If you like the sound of a laid-back exhibition space/café with an eclectic music playlist – they have an album of the month too – this should be an enjoyable snack stop. Good cappuccini, panini and sandwiches with wacky names, as well as soups. Exhibits and sells works of new artists, including graduates of Glasgow and London schools of art. Comfy sofas are ideal for a sociable, extended luncheon.

East End *p31, map p26*

£ Café Source, 1 St Andrews Sq, in the church, T0141-548 6020, www.standrews inthesquare.com. Open daily till late. Superb contemporary café-bar housed in a Scots cultural centre, offering everything from traditional fishcakes and Scotch pies to more exotic creations such as oak-smoked salmon bagels and savoury vegetarian tarts. Seasonal Scots produce like West Coast mussels and Highland beef get an outing too. It's a good spot to enjoy a decent coffee while perusing the papers. Live music and Ceilidh dance classes every Wed from 2100.

West End and along the Clyde *p39 and p46, maps p40 and p42*

£££ La Parmigiana, 443 Great Western Rd, T0141-334 0686, www.laparmigiana.co.uk. Closed Sun after 1800. This sophisticated Italian restaurant is one of Glasgow's finest eating establishments and a firm favourite for over 35 years. La famiglia Giovanni have served elegant Italian dishes to many celebs and west-enders. They make their own fresh egg pasta in creations such as seafood tagliolini and farfalle with sausages. Standout *secondi* (mains) include: organic Scots salmon with leeks and lemon; and guinea fowl with porcini mushrooms and a rosemary and grappa sauce. Recommended for a special occasion.

£££ Two Fat Ladies at the The Buttery, 652 Argyle St, T0141-221 8188, twofatladiesrestaurant.com. Closed Mon. Dark wood Victoriana abounds in this old favourite with its warm atmosphere. Consistently rated as one of the best in the city, with an emphasis on the finest Scottish fish, seafood and game. A standout dish is the flash-fried west coast scallops with sweet potato and coriander puree, and pancetta cream.

£££ Ubiquitous Chip, 12 Ashton La, T0141-334 5007, www.ubiquitouschip.co.uk. Daily. A groundbreaking restaurant and Glasgow institution for over 40 years, housed in a converted mews stable. The colourful surroundings – with murals by Alasdair Gray – are the backdrop to cultural events and many an arty conversation. There's a leafy cobbled yard with glass canopy while upstairs the brasserie serves cheaper but still elegant mains, pieces (sandwiches) and platters. For a special occasion dine in the main restaurant which uses the best Scots produce in imaginative dishes such as grilled haunch of Carspairn roe deer with chocolate crumb, and Atlantic halibut with crispy chicken wings. Aberdeen Angus beef and an array of artisan cheeses are mainstays. Pre-theatre and set menus start at £16 for 2 courses.

££ Ashoka West End, 1284 Argyle St, T0141-339 3371, www.ashokarestaurants. com. This may be the oldest in this everpopular chain of Indians, but it gets mixed reviews these days and seems more geared to takeaways. The intimate surroundings can feel a tad claustrophobic at weekends. There are plenty of vegetarian-friendly options.

££ Balbir's, 7 Church St, T0141-339 7711, www.balbirsrestaurants.co.uk. Daily dinner only from 1700. Don't be put off by the rather soulless exterior – this much-loved Glasgow curry house favourite has the added bonus that their fresh ingredients make it a healthy choice. The tandoori salmon, hand spiced and coal-oven roasted is a revelation. There's a plethora of choices for vegetarians and carnivores alike. Food is prepared in cholesterol-free oil and no artificial colours or additives are used.

££ Brel, 39-43 Ashton La, T0141-342 4966, www.brelbarrestaurant.com. Daily till 2400. Another stylish Continental eating establishment in Glasgow's hippest culinary quarter. This time it's Belgian and they are big on mussels (*moules marinière*), smoky sausages and quality beer, including many Belgian brews. They also do chowder, seafood linguine, fish and chips, burgers and salads. Pub atmosphere popular with groups.

££ Butchershop, 1055 Sauchiehall St, T0141-339 2999, www.butchershopglasgow. com. Daily till late. New York-style bistro with some Gallic influence that serves quality dry-aged beef steaks, T-bones, sirloins and chunky burgers with frites, as well as bountiful seafood platters, Atlantic cod, risottos, quality wines and cocktails. They also do set Sunday roasts, pre-theatre, kids and set lunch menus.

££ The Cabin, 996-998 Dumbarton Rd, T0141-569 1036, www.cabinglasgow.com. Closed Mon. Pre-theatre menu 1700-1900. If your idea of a good night out is piles of the finest Scottish food in a nautically themed space, followed by a post-dinner cabaret, then this is the place for you. A truly one-off experience and great fun for small groups especially; the only drawback is there's only 1 entertainment sitting, at 1930 Sat. Expect quality produce such as fillet of beef Wellington, lemon sole and breast of Barbary duck.

££ Grassroots Café, 97 St George's Rd, T0141-333 0534, www.grassrootsorganic. co.uk. Opened in the 1970s Grassroots Organic was a pioneer in championing, growing and serving vegetarian and vegan food. The shop and intimate café near St George's Cross continues to dish up lots of healthy soups, salads and filling main courses. It's a tad pricey though these days so don't expect the wholesome bargains of yesteryear.

££ Mother India, 28 Westminster Terr, Sauchiehall St, T0141-221 1663, www. motherindiaglasgow.co.uk. Mon-Wed 1730-2230, Fri-Sat 1200-2300, Sun 1200-2200. Exquisite home-style 'desi' Indian cooking at affordable prices that consistently gets great reviews. The best bet for an Indian in the West End since 1996. There are 3 floors with different atmospheres from the cosy ground-floor area with a street view to a theatrical, intimate cellar and the dark wood-panelled main dining room. Renowned for a friendly and informal atmosphere. There's a healthy vegetarian selection. Great value set lunch and good banquet menus.

££ Mr Singh's India, 149 Elderslie St, T0141-204 0186, www.mistersinghsindia.com. Mon-Sat 1200-2400, Sun 1430-2400. Imagine good Punjabi cooking brought to you by kilted waiters with a background wallpaper of disco music. As well as classic Indian dishes such as balti, masala and korma, they offer their secret signature dish, Ambala, swordfish tandoori and haggis pakora. Bright contemporary decor with Indian tiles and exotic sculptural wood. Popular with local celebs and Rangers players so you never know who will pop in for a popadum. It's very child friendly. Check website for latest cookery classes and demos.

££ Shish Mahal, 66-68 Park Rd, T0141-334 7899, www.shishmahal.co.uk. Daily lunch and dinner, Fri-Sat all day, Sun 1700-2400. 'The Shish' has long been a byword for great curry in Glasgow. The Pakistani food's imaginative and there's loads of choice. Contemporary dining areas with atmospheric lighting and some bespoke touches that recall Pakistan.

££ Stravaigin, 28-30 Gibson St, T0141-334 2665, www.stravaigin.co.uk. Daily. Book a table in the atmospheric basement for a sophisticated yet relaxed dining experince. Known for the eclectic mix of flavours and prime Scottish ingredients, and wins plaudits for its top-class cuisine at affordable prices. Menu full of Scots meats such as char-grilled steaks and haggis – and seasonal seafood such as mussels and monkfish. Upstairs is a café-bar where you can sample some of that fabulous food at even more affordable prices. Various set menus provide greatest value. Stages culinary and cultural events; check the website for details.

£ The Bay Tree, 403 Great Western Rd, T0141-334 5898, www.baytreecafe.com. Mon-Sat 0900-2200; Sun 0900-2100. Long-established (since 1960) café serving food with a Middle Eastern and Mediterranean emphasis. Expect Turkish- and Greek-style lamb, Persian kebabs and pasta dishes. There's a selection of vegetarian and vegan plates. Live piano and Arabic music most week nights. No wine available so best bring your own.

Cafés

Grosvenor Café, 31 Ashton La, T0141-339 1848, www.grosvenorcafe.co.uk. Generally 1200-2300, till 0100 Fri-Sat. Housed in the handsome old **Grosvenor** cinema behind Hillhead Underground. A perennial favourite with students and locals who come for the wide selection of good value food (filled rolls, soup, burgers, pizzas, etc). Balcony overlooking Ashton Lane is a popular hangout in the summer months. Next door is the **Vinyl Bar** which has snacks, cocktails and eclectic music policy. Check website for latest cinema (lots of art house flicks) and cultural events.

Little Italy, 205 Byres Rd, T0141-339 6287, www.littleitalyglasgow.com. Mon-Thu 0800-2200, Fri and Sat 0800-0100, Sun 1000-2200. It's a busy refuelling stop with Italian-themed decor and diner seating. Delivers good-value pizza and focaccia, cheap pasta dishes, heaped salads and espresso to go.

North Star, 108 Queen Margaret Dr, T0141-946 5365. Mon-Sat 0800-1800, Sun 1000-1700. Italian café/deli with an extremely loyal following, who come to enjoy friendly Puglian hospitality and Scots-Italian fare. Expect tasty omlettes, pasta dishes and Italian cakes including orange and polenta *torta*. They do excellent vegetarian options and kids' portions.

University Café, 87 Byres Rd, T0141-339 5217. Mon-Thu 0900-2200, Fri and Sat 0900-2230, Sun 1000-2200. Legendary Italian art deco, formica-filled caff, where grannies and students sit shoulder-to-shoulder enjoying real cappuccino, great ice cream and good, honest and cheap mince and tatties, pie and chips and all the other golden oldies. A glorious evocation of a world before sundried tomatoes.

South Side p49, map p26

££ Ashoka Southside, 268 Clarkston Rd, T0141-637 0711, www.ashokasouthside.info. Fri and Sat 1700-2400, Sun-Thu 1700-2300. Small and intimate Southside version of this venerable chain of Indian restaurants – and arguably the most reliably good dining experience of the lot. Check website for latest deals including 30% off bill Tue and Wed.

££ Edwardian Kitchen Restaurant, Pollock House, 2060 Pollokshaws Rd, T0141-616 6410. Daily 1000-1700. The grand basement restaurant housed in the old Pollok House kitchen serves contemporary Scots cuisine and hearty vegetarian dishes. For a treat try their delicious cakes, scones and tea beloved of Glasgow ladies of leisure.

££ Spice Garden, 11-17 Clyde Pl, T0141-429 4422, www.spicegarden.com. Daily 1800-0330.There's an enormous choice at this popular Indian restaurant, from tandooris

and biryanis to European dishes like pizzas, steaks and chicken kiev. It's conveniently open all night so good for those desperate for a post-club curry.

££ Wee Cucina, 205 Fenwick Rd, Giffnock, T0141-621 1903, www.weecucina.com. Mon-Sat 1200-2200, Sun 1600-2200. Occupying the old **Cook's Room** this intimate place has added an emphasis on Italian food amid contemporary surroundings. You can relax in the comfy banquette seating and peruse a menu full of pasta and risotto dishes, meat and seafood. There's a choice of child-friendly small plates they call *piccoli piatti*: mini pizzas and focaccias. There's a fabulous choice of vegetarian options and good-value set menus.

£ Buongiorno, 1021 Pollokshaws Rd, T0141-649 1029, www.buongiorno.org.uk. Mon-Sat 1100-2300, Sun 1100-2200. A comfortable and welcoming contemporary diner-style eatery serving simple Italian food and excellent breakfasts at very reasonable prices. Expect decent pizza margheritas, choice of vegetarian-friendly antipasti and homemade tiramisu. It's very popular for the superb-value lunch and early evening set-menu (1700-1900) deals.

£ The Glad Café, 1006a Pollokshaws Rd, T0141-636 6119, www.thegladcafe.co.uk. Fabulous café in Shawlands that serves wholesome fare – like beef stew with horseradish dumplings – alongside, snacks, sharing platters and vegetarian dishes. Home baking, Green Roast coffee and a wide choice of breakfasts are also available. Check out the live music events here too; see page 76.

£ Greek Golden Kebab, 34 Sinclair Dr, T0141-649 7581, www.greekgoldenkebab.com. Thu-Sun 1700-0100. Established in 1972 and run by the friendly Kyriacou family, this place has an alluringly kitsch interior with lots of 70s wood-panelling. Expect plentiful home cooked Greek food at reasonable prices. Lots of vegetarian options and a takeaway service too.

£ Tramway Café-Bar, 25 Albert Dr, T0141-276 0953, www.tramway.org. Tue-Sat 0900-

1700, Sun 1200-1700. A contemporary space looking onto Tramway art centre's beautiful Hidden Gardens. Serves superb vegetarian and pasta dishes, burgers and sandwiches.

Cafés

Art Lovers' Café, Bellahouston Park, Drumbreck Rd, T0141-353 4779, www. houseforanartlover.co.uk. Daily 1000-1700. Housed in the exquisite Rennie Mackintosh-designed House for an Art Lover (see page 50). A wonderful place to relax with a good selection of light snacks and elegant hot and cold meals. Expect a choice of seafood, chicken, venison and pork, vegetarian options and a couple of tempting desserts. Contemporary art exhibitions are displayed in the relaxing dining room. When the sun comes out the sunny multi-layered terrace overlooking the gardens is a great place for people watching.

Around Glasgow *p53*

££ Ristorante La Vigna, 40 Wellgate, Lanark, T0141-630351, www.lavigna.co.uk. Closed Sun lunch. The traditional Italian with its dated but homely interior has been popular with locals and visitors since opening back in 1983. Standout pasta dishes include duck ravioli with whipped butter, sage, pancetta and Parmesan and the grilled lobster with squid-ink spaghetti and seafood (perfect for a couple). Ask about the excellent lunch and evening set menu specials.

££ Scrib Tree, 1 Colliers Court, Douglas, Lanark, T01555-851262, www.thescribtree. co.uk. Mon-Fri 0800-1800 (closed Wed), Sat-Sun 1000-1600. Pristine café-restaurant with a wonderful farm shop full of fresh produce based on the Douglas Estate. Expect lots of locally grown and sourced food including lamb, beef and game from the estate, vegetables from the Hirsel Estate and oven-hot bread and cakes from Alexander Taylor of Strathaven nearby. It's an excellent choice for quality Italian ground coffee and home-baked cakes, light snack and hearty meals.

🍸 Bars and clubs

Forget all the tired old clichés about Glasgow and Glaswegians, a night out in Scotland's largest city is a memorable experience – for all the right reasons. Glasgow is bursting at the seams with bars, pubs and music venues to suit all tastes from ornate Victorian watering holes to the coolest music venues and multilevel clubs. There's a plethora of designer bars, where a dressed-up crowds listen to banging dance beats before heading off to a mainstream club. Glasgow's fertile music and arts scene provides an eclectic array of venues playing different kinds of music from reggae to house to indie to dubstep. Some places do themed nights with quirky fancy dress, others have live music followed by a club. Most pubs and bars open till 2400, though a few are open later, and many of them close at 2300 on weekdays and Sun. DJs normally start at 2100 till 2400 and entry is usually free, with some places charging after 2300 when they transform into clubs.

One of the best areas for the sheer number and variety of pubs and bars is the West End, with its large student population. The city centre has a great choice too with all the music and fashion tribes catered for in and around Sauciehall St. A number of style bars line Bath St and Glasgow's gay scene has grown around the trendy bars and cafés of the Merchant City, especially Virginia St, Wilson St and Glassford St. See also Live music, page 75.

Glasgow's club scene, much of which is found in the city centre, is amongst the most vibrant in the UK. Opening times are pretty much the same all over with doors opening from 2300-0300. Entry costs vary from £4-10 for smaller clubs and up to £25 for some of the special club nights with big-name DJs.

Glasgow's music and arts crossover

Glasgow has a thriving arts and music scene, a vitality that is much celebrated for its collaborative DIY spirit. During the deep recession and sectarian violence of late 1970s and early 80s, a nascent music and arts scene embraced that punk spirit. Obsession with exotic sounds, uplifting Motown beats and jangly West Coast pop squeezed Edwyn Collins' Orange Juice from bedroom to national consciousness on *Top of the Pops*. Homespun fanzines, cassettes, record labels and music venues put the city on the musical map. A succession of bands including The Pastels, Jesus and Mary Chain, Primal Scream, Teenage Fan Club, Mogwai and Camera Obscura have followed.

Meanwhile, inspired by this spirit and the legacy of the Glasgow School of Art alumni, New Glasgow Boys and Girls occupied the city's empty warehouse spaces establishing gallery collectives including Transmission, which was established in 1983. By the mid-90s and into the noughties contemporary art was mainstream fodder and Glasgow opened showcase galleries and arts hubs including GoMA (**Gallery of Modern Art**), **CCA** (**Centre of Contemporary Art**) and **Trongate 103**. The **Glasgow International Visual Arts Festival** now attracts the international art set and Glasgow-based artists keep winning the Turner Prize. The ever-influential **GSA** (**Glasgow School of Art**) has just added a striking contemporary wing to its iconic Charles Rennie Mackintosh building. Spurred by this DIY spirit and the impetus generated by being 1990 European Capital of Culture, restaurants and other businesses have transformed the Merchant City into a smart area to work and play. Government-led public-private partnerships seek to continue this urban renewal along Trongate, King Street and towards the Clyde.

Glasgow's music fans and art students still start bands, galleries, and record labels. DJ duo Slam mined Teutonic beats and Detroit techno founding Soma Quality Recordings in 1991, while Optimo celebrated vinyl pick and mix. The dance and electronic scene still evolves at the legendary **Sub Club**, **Arches** and newer **SWG3** and creating LuckyMe collective artists Hudson Mohawke and Rustie.

Contemporary arts aficionados should start at **CCA** while music lovers must head to **Monorail**; a record shop, café and venue rolled into one. Among the vinyl racks you'll find releases on labels such as Mogwai's *Rock Action*, *Chemikal Underground*, *Optimo* and *Watts of Goodwill*. Pick up fliers and info from the counter about the city's post-industrial spaces turned arts/music venues such as **The Arches**, **Trongate 103**, **Tramway**, **Stereo** and **Flying Duck**.

Monorail and Watts Of Goodwill record label owner Dep Downey knows all the about the Glasgow scene and what makes it special: "I think it's a small enough city for everybody to get to get to know each other. I've yet to witness any hierarchy between bands. I'm sure the weather plays a factor in encouraging creativity and gig attendance. There are always crossovers happening in the music and art scenes. They are so intertwined. You only have to check how many current and ex-art students are playing in bands".

Dep Downey's (Monorail) essential Glasgow albums are: Jesus and Mary Chain *Psychocandy* (Blanco y Negro) from the 1980s; Teenage Fanclub *Bandwagonesque* (Creation) from the 1990s; Alasdair Roberts *The Crook of My Arm* (Secretly Canadian) from the 2000s; and, post-2010, RM Hubbert *13 Lost and Found* (Chemikal Underground).

City centre, Buchanan St and Sauciehall St *p24, p34 and p37, map p26*

Bars

Babbity Bowster, see page 60. Prime Merchant City pub that has everything; lively atmosphere, wide selection of real ales and good food.

Bar Ten, 10 Mitchell St, T0141-572 1448, http://navantaverns.com/bar10. A narrow European-style bar in a converted warehouse with shiny surfaces and changing art works on the walls. After 20 years, it's still a popular pre-club destination and hosts soul nights.

Blackfriars, 36 Bell St, T0141-552 5924, www.blackfriarsglasgow.com. Merchant city favourite which pulls in the punters with its vast range of international beers and lagers. Also a wide range of excellent grub, live music and comedy at weekends and that inimitable Glasgow atmosphere. See also Entertaiment, page 76.

Bloc, 117 Bath St, T0141-574 6066, www.bloc.ru/barbloc.html. A studenty bar with an eclectic live music policy. Diner food on the menu including burgers, pizza and pasta dishes.

Flying Duck, 142 Renfield St, T0141-564 1540, www.flyingduckclub.com. Cool bar and club with 1970s furniture surrounding the dancefloor. Quirky club nights, live bands, themed fancy dress evenings, film-based nights and art classes – including Lebowski-fest and Back Tae Mine featuring Gavin Dunbar (Camera Obscura) and guest DJs. Free toast, board games and other treats add to the house-party vibe.

The Griffin, 226 Bath St, T0141-331 5170, thegriffinglasgow.co.uk. Opposite the **King's Theatre**. Turn-of-the-century pub (not the most recent one). Bar menu includes pie and chips plus vegetarian dishes.

The Horse Shoe Bar, 17 Drury St, T0141-248 6368, www.horseshoebar.co.uk. Classic Victorian Gin Palace with lots of character and original features – between Mitchell St and Renfield St, near the station. Its much-copied island bar is the longest continuous bar in the UK, so it shouldn't take long to get served, which is fortunate as it gets very busy. Good-value food served and one of the cheapest pints in town. If you only visit one pub during your stay, then make sure it's this one.

The Pot Still, 154 Hope St, T0141-333 0980, thepotstill.co.uk. Edwardian traditional pub justly famous for its massive range of malts (around 500 of them). They also have a selection of cask ales and decent pub grub during the day.

The Victoria Bar, 159 Bridgegate, T0141-552 6040. Real traditional howff in one of Glasgow's oldest streets. Seemingly unchanged since the late 19th century and long may it stay that way. One of the city's great pubs, where entertainment – including folk music – is provided free, courtesy of the local wags.

Clubs

Alaska, 142 Bath La, T0141-248 1777. Everything from funk and soul to house music.

Archaos, 25 Queen St, T0141-204 3189. A younger more dressy crowd come here for house, techno and club classics in this massive venue.

Arches, 253 Argyle St, T0901-022 0300, www.thearches.co.uk. Cavernous space under Central station. A legendary arts venue and club featuring the cutting edge of the UK dance scene. Also holds live music events and stages theatre performances, see pages 76 and 77.

The Garage, 490 Sauchiehall St, T0141-332 1120, www.garageglasgow.co.uk. Student haunt featuring cheesy clubs nights, live bands (see page 77) and occasional comedy nights.

The Sub Club, 22 Jamaica St, T0141-248 4600, www.subclub.co.uk. One of the city's favourite dance/techno clubs has a state-of-the-art soundsystem and Bodysonic dancefloor these days. It's often voted among the best club atmospheres in the UK by *Mixmag*. Check website for latest DJ line-ups for legendary nights Slam, Subculture, and Twitch and Wilkes' Optimo, an eclectic mix for music hedonists.

The Tunnel, 84 Mitchell St, T0141-204 1000, www.tunnelglasgow.co.uk. Mainstream dance music club going strong for over 20 years.

Gay venues

Delmonica's, 68 Virginia St, T0141-552 4803, www.delmonicas.co.uk. Daily 1200-2400. Free. Opened in 1991, this stylish contemporary gay club has lots of themed nights and a loyal, up-for-it crowd. Check website for latest events.

Merchant Pride, 20 Candleriggs, T0141-564 1285. Mon-Sun 1200-2400. Sociable bar with karaoke nights and jazz sessions on Sat.

Underground, 6a John St, T0141 553 2456, www.underground-glasgow.com. Friendly gay bar in the throbbing heart of the Merchant City's so-called 'Pink Triangle' – playing chart music and the odd alternative tune.

West End and along the Clyde *p39 and p46, map p40*

Black Sparrow, 241 North St, T0141-221 5530, www.theblacksparrow.co.uk. Named after Charles Bukowski's publishing company this theme bar is renowned for its excellent bar food – check out the burgers and tapas deals – plus entertainment nights including quizzes and DJ nights.

Butchershop, 1055 Sauchiehall St, T0141-339 2999, www.butchershopglasgow.com. Sophisticated bar and grill popular with an older crowd. They serve quality dry-aged beef steaks and burgers, as well as seafood platters, quality wines and cocktails.

Dram! 232 Woodlands Rd, T0141-332 1622, www.dramglasgow.co.uk. Smart pub with exposed brick, dozens of malts and decent food, including stone-baked haggis and jalapeño pizza. Features Sky Sports 3D and can get rammed when big games are on.

Firebird, 1321 Argyle St, www.firebird glasgow.com. A stylish bar with a timeless feel serving excellent Mediterranean and Morrocan-influenced food plus a choice of changing microbrewery beers. Imagine a family-friendly space with huge windows and pizzas from a wood-fired oven.

The Halt Bar, 160 Woodlands Rd, T0141-353 6450. This erstwhile tram stop (hence the name) is one of Glasgow's great unspoiled pubs with many of the original Edwardian fixtures intact. Check out the vibrant arts scene here including comedy nights, live music and DJ sets.

Lock 27, 1100 Crow Rd, T0141-958 0853, www.lock27.com. If the weather's fine (and it sometimes is), there are few bonnier places to enjoy a spot of al fresco eating and drinking than this pub by the Forth and Clyde Canal in Anniesland. There's a decent food menu – mainly salads, soup, seafood, chicken and vegetarian – served and kids are made welcome. You could take a stroll along the towpath afterwards.

Òran Mór, top of Byres Rd, near Botanic Gardens, T0141-357 6200, www.oran-mor. co.uk. The former Kelvinside church is now a fabulous arts venue offering a couple of atmospheric bars, the cavernous auditorium with towering Alasdair Gray murals and a brasserie. Popular beer garden when the sun appears. Well worth popping in to see the interiors and check the latest events or check the website. Brasserie bar is open till 0300 daily. See also page 77.

SWG3 & Poetry Club, 100 Eastvale Pl, T0141-357 7246, www.swg3.tv. **Poetry Club** is an intimate bar and performance space that came about through arts collaboration between artist Jim Lambie and punk pioneer Richard Hell. SWG3's larger Warehouse stages regular events including club nights; see page 77. Check the latest listings for its cross-cultural programme of music, poetry and theatre. Well worth a trip west to meet some interesting, talented people and to view the Poetry Club's Flying Scotsman smoke machine.

Tennent's, 191 Byres Rd, T0141-339 7203, www.thetennentsbarglasgow.co.uk. Spacious no-nonsense, old West End favourite, serving a range of fine ales to a genuinely mixed crowd. They have a grill (check out the burger and pint deal), show live sports and have basement events including quiz and DJs nights in the basement.

South Side *p49, map p26*

Samuel Dow's, 69-71 Nithsdale Rd, T0141-423 0107. Or **Sammy Dow's** as it's known by its many Shawlands regulars. A friendly Southside local serving good ale and cheap bar food. Check the *List* magazine for latest live rock bands and jam nights.

Waverley Tea Room, 18 Moss Side Rd, T0845-659 5903, www.waverleytearoom. co.uk. Family-orientated tea room by day and homely bar by night with late licence till 0100 weekdays and 0200 on the weekend. Good for families.

Clubs

Glasgow Grand Ole Opry, 2-4 Govan Rd, T0141-429 5396, www.glasgowsgrandole opry.co.uk. Legendary country and western club packing them in since 1974. Housed in a handsome former 1920s cinema, the club is attended by old-timers and young bucks who dig the country sounds and dance classes: line and jive mainly.

☻ Entertainment

Glasgow *p20, maps p22, p26, p40 and p42*
20-odd years since Glasgow was European City of Culture (1990) the city continues to invent a wide span of art, theatre, film and music. The majority of the larger theatres, concert halls and cinemas are concentrated in the city centre, though its 2 most renowned theatres, the **Citizens'** and the **Tramway**, are to be found south of the Clyde. Keep an eye on the many smaller independent venues like **Mono**, **Flying Duck** and **Stereo** in and around the Merchant City, South Side's **Glad Café** and the West End's **Òran Mór** and **Poetry Club** for an eclectic mix of cultural events. Glasgow's

many cultural festivals, including **Glasgow International Arts (GI)** also throw up exciting pop-up venues from time-to-time. *Glasgow Life* (www.glasgowlife.org.uk) lists the latest events.

Details of all the city's events are also listed in the 2 local newspapers, *The Herald* and *Evening Times*. Another excellent source of information is the fortnightly listings magazine and online resource *The List*, www.list.co.uk, which also covers Edinburgh and which is on sale in most newsagents. *The Skinny* magazine is good for the latest alternative events. To book tickets for concerts or theatre productions, call at the **Ticket Centre**, City Hall, Candleriggs, Mon-Sat 0900-1800; Sun 1200-1700. Phone bookings T0141-2874000, Mon-Sat 0900-2100; Sun 0900-1800. Many of the live music venues don't have their own box offices these days, and booking is online or via premium rate telephone. The main agencies that sell rock and pop tickets include: **SEE Tickets**, T0871-2200260, www.seetickets. com, **Ticketmaster**, T0844-847 1697, www. ticketmaster.co.uk, **Gigantic**, www.gigantic. com, and **Tickets Scotland Glasgow**, T0141-204 5151, www.tickets-scotland.com.

Cinema

Glasgow has mainstream multiplexes throughout the city and a few art house cinemas. Some intimate arts centres and venues also screen quirky, foreign-language and short films by emerging filmmakers.
Cineworld Glasgow, 7 Renfrew St, T0871-200 2000, www.cineworld.co.uk. 18-screens and the city's busiest cinema complex, and the world's tallest at 170 ft. Take the great glass elevator for some cinematic views.
The Glad Café, 1006a Pollokshaws Rd, T0141-636 6119, www.thegladcafe.co.uk. An eclectic programme of films run by the Southside Film Club.
Glasgow Film Theatre (GFT), 12 Rose St, T0141-332 6535, www.glasgowfilm.org. Hosts the **Glasgow Film Festival**. Expect an excellent programme of art house movies

and a bar for discussion later. It's one of Britain's most beautiful custom-built art deco (1939) cinemas and a must-visit for movie and architecture buffs.

Grosvenor, Ashton La, off Byres Rd in the West End, T0141-339 8444. An old refurbished 2-screen cinema, showing art house and mainstream films.

Mono, Kings Court, King St, T0141-553 2400, www.monocafebar.com. Art-house and foreign-language cinema in an intimate cultural venue.

Comedy

Blackfriars, 36 Bell St, T0141-552 5924, www.blackfriarsglasgow.com. Regular comedy nights and a venue during the **Glasgow Comedy Festival**. Also live music and real cask ales. Check website for latest listings.

Stand Comedy Club, 333 Woodlands Rd, T0844-335 8879, www.thestand.co.uk. Glasgow outpost of the legendary comedy club housed in an old school basement – it's open 7 nights a week. Friendly atmosphere (stag nights are banned) and expect lots of talent from near and far. It's where many big acts try out new material. Check website for latest gigs.

The State Bar, 148 Holland St, T0141-3322159. Good comedy club on Sat nights. Also live blues on Tue and a good selection of real ales. Not a bad pub too.

Concerts

These are the main concert venues, but don't forget that Glasgow is full of smaller independent clubs and cultural hubs: see also Live music, below.

City Halls, Candleriggs, T0141-353 8000, www.glasgowconcerthalls.com. Smaller-scale classical, jazz and folk music events. It's the Glasgow home of the Scottish Chamber Orchestra.

Glasgow Royal Concert Hall, 2 Sauchiehall St, T0141-353 8080, www.grch.com. Prestigious venue for orchestras and big-name rock, pop and soul acts.

Henry Wood Hall, 73 Claremont St, T0141-225 3555, www.rsno.org.uk. HQ of the Royal Scottish National Orchestra.

O2 ABC, 300 Sauchiehall St, T0844-477 2000, www.o2abcglasgow.co.uk. Fantastic place for live music in a converted cinema. Check the website for a packed programme of pop, indie and dance acts from all over the world. The main hall hosts the main concerts while the **ABC2** does the small gigs and club nights.

Old Fruitmarket, Candleriggs, T0141-353 8000, www.glasgowconcerthalls.com/oldfruitmarket. The old fruit and veg market next the **City Halls** has lots of original mercantile features, and hosts a varied programme music and cultural events.

Royal Scottish Conservatoire, 100 Renfrew St, T0141-332 4101,www.rcs.ac.uk. Former RSAMD (Royal Scottish Academy of Music and Drama) has a varied programme of international performances and student productions. Also hosts lunchtime concerts.

SECC (Scotttish Exhibition and Conference Centre), Exhibition Way, West End, T0141-248 3000, www.secc.co.uk. Known as the **Armadillo**, this striking Clydeside venue is the place for big name pop, rock and hippity-hop acts.

St Andrew's in the Square, 1 St. Andrew's in the Square, near Glasgow Cross, T0141-559 5902, www.standrewsinthesquare.com. A handsomely restored 18th-century church which is now a centre of Scottish culture and stages traditional music concerts and dance classes.

Theatre Royal, Hope St, T0141-332 3321. The home of the generally excellent Scottish Opera and Scottish Ballet, also regularly hosts large-scale touring theatre and dance companies and orchestras. It's the oldest theatre in Glasgow and recently underwent a striking revamp.

Live music

Arches Café Bar, see page 73. Part of the legendary arts centre and club, you can rely on this place to deliver an excellent line-up of well-regarded alternative acts and bands from James Blake to the Handsome Family.

Barrowlands, Gallowgate, T0141-552 4601. Famous old East End ballroom and now Glasgow's liveliest and best-loved gig venue. Popular with acts breaking through and big names trying to rediscover what it's about. Great atmosphere dripping with condensation when packed.

Clutha Vaults, 167 Stockwell St, T0141-552 7520. Long-established pub which has live music near the Clyde.

Cottier's, 93-95 Hyndland St, T0141-357 5825, www.cottiers.com. Intimate venue for more esoteric music acts, also jazz, classical and blues.

The Garage, 490 Sauchiehall St, T0141-332 1120, www.garageglasgow.co.uk. Medium-sized venue for bands on the verge of a breakthrough. A few bands to pass through the doors are CSS, New York Dolls, Prince, Kasabian and Tinchy Stryder.

The Glad Café, 1006a Pollokshaws Rd, T0141-636 6119, www.thegladcafe.co.uk. Intimate café and bar with a 100-capacity venue that hosts film nights and top music acts from electronica acts like Loscil to Americana-influenced bands and local experimenters like Withered Hand. Dep Downey of record shop/venue **Monorail** says it's one of his favourite Glasgow venues.

King Tut's Wah Wah Hut, 272a St Vincent St, T0141-221 5279. Glasgow's hallowed live music venue. Many a famous band has made the break in this cramped, sweaty club. Good bar downstairs for a pre-gig drink.

Mono, Kings Court, King St, T0141-553 2400, www.monocafebar.com. Small gigs by interesting bands and alternative artists make this music/arts/record shop a muso favourite.

Nice 'n' Sleazy, 421 Sauchiehall St, T0141-333 0900, www.nicensleazy.com. Great bar and music venue with an eclectic mix of people and music. The upstairs bar is a favourite with musos who take advantage of the fine jukebox, while downstairs hosts Indie gigs and club nights. Check out the website for the latest listings.

Òran Mór, see page 74. Excellent music gigs featuring international artists, club nights, comedy slots and other cultural events. Always an eclectic line-up and superb setting. Expect Indie acts, established artists and emerging talent like British Sea Power, Lana del Rey, Saint Etienne and Everything Everything.

Scottish Exhibition and Conference Centre (SECC), Finnieston Quay, T0141-248 3000, www.secc.co.uk. Cavernous and soulless multi-purpose venue – it has all the atmosphere of a disused aircraft hangar. This is the venue for big name acts cashing in. Catchy nickname captures its metallic carapace profile: the Armadillo.

Stereo/Hairdressers, 22-28 Renfield La, T0141-222 2254, www.stereocafebar.com. Superb basement music venue that stages alternative gigs – from the latest BBC 6 Music-trumpeted bands to local old timers like Vic Godard and international Indie heroes like Howe Gelb. Good club nights and vegan café too. **Hairdressers** also does gigs and comedy nights.

SWG3 & Poetry Club, 100 Eastvale Pl, T0141-357 7246, www.swg3.tv. Part of the massive **SWGE (Studio Warehouse Glasgow** arts centre) these 2 spaces stage an array of alternative live acts, DJ set and collaborative arty events.

Theatre

The Arches, 30 Midland St, T0141-565 1000, www.thearches.co.uk. Iconic arts venue under the railway arches of Central station. Presents more radical and experimental theatre. Also home to some of the city's major club nights, see Clubs, page 73.

Centre for Contemporary Arts (CCA), 350 Sauchiehall St, T0141-352 4900, www.cca-glasgow.com. Arts venue that hosts contemporary dance, music and theatre, as well as staging various art exhibitions.

Citizens' Theatre, 119 Gorbals St, T0141-429 0022, www.citz.co.uk. Just across the river, this much-loved luvvie home stages some of the UK's most exciting and innovative drama. Beyond the striking glass façade is a plush red Victorian space where well-known Scots and International actors mix with emerging talent. As well as the evocative main auditorium there are 2 smaller studios that also stage experimental productions and various classes. There are generous discounts for students and the unemployed.

King's Theatre, 297 Bath St, T0141-240 1300. Imposing red-brick edifice built in 1904 and Glasgow's main traditional theatre presenting musicals, panto, comedy and all sorts of popular turns.

Mitchell Theatre, 6 Granville St, T0141-287 2999. Stately theatre at Charing Cross that stages various drama productions as well as occasional jazz concerts.

Theatre Royal, see above. Primarily a concert hall this recently refurbished theatre also stages high and middle brow theatre.

Tramway Theatre, 25 Albert Dr, T0845-330 3501, www.tramway.org. Internationally renowned venue in a converted tram depot with a varied programme of innovative and influential theatre, dance, music and art exhibitions. You need to head South Side, just off Pollokshaws Rd. **Tramway** has a wonderful garden and café too (see page 70).

Tron Theatre, 63 Trongate, T0141-552 4267, www.tron.co.uk. Part of an emerging creative hub along the Trongate and the Merchant City (see page 29), the Tron is housed in an old kirk and contemporary building. Expect major contemporary theatre productions, musical performances and big-name comedy acts. It's also home to a fine bar and restaurant; see page 66.

O Shopping

Glasgow p20, maps p22, p26, p40 and p42
Glasgow is a shopaholic's paradise – particularly for anyone seeking clothes. Locals love fashion and are happy to spend their money on good clobber – so were staggered when **Harvey Nicks** chose to locate their first Scottish store in staid old Edinburgh rather than streetwise Glasgow. Despite that snub, Glasgow is still the best shopping city in the UK after London and there are endless opportunities for retail therapy.

Merchant City is the city's most upmarket shopping area with some stylish restaurants and cafés to rest your fistfuls of chic designer bags. Fashionistas should firstly click their exquisitely clad feet over to the classy Italian Centre and then explore the grid of streets and converted tobacco warehouses such as Merchant Square and Virginia Court. Buchanan St is the most upmarket of the city's central retail thoroughfares, while cheaper outlets are focused on Sauchiehall St and Argyle St. Argyll Arcade is a covered heaven for jewellery janglers seeking new and antique shiny, sparkling things. West Regent St is the place to go for antiques and art, with Victorian Village is a behemoth of gallery finds. There are some sizeable shopping centres too, like the Buchanan Galleries near Queen St Station, which has a large branch of the **John Lewis** department store, as well as all the usual high street suspects. There's also the ever-classy Princes Sq, which has a good mix of designer stores, gift shops and refreshment pit-stops. Often overlooked is the area round King St, which has loads of individual galleries and is a great place for anyone looking for contemporary artworks to take home. The West End is the place to go for more off-beat and quirky purchases, with designer jewellers, vintage and independent clothes shops, and second-hand bookshops. Head down cobbled Ashton, Cresswell and Ruthven Lanes to rummage through 20th-century antiques, vintage clothing and quirky gifts. Then there's the Barras, an indoor market east of the Merchant City where you can find everything from bric-a-brac, textiles, antique and faux-auld furniture and trinkets, with collectable goodies amid the clutter and counterfeits.

City Centre and Merchant City *p24, map p22*

Books, music and games
Aye-Aye, 350 Sauchiehall St, T07946-643757, www.aye-ayebooks.com. Art bookshop in the CCA foyer. The place to find obscure magazines and limited editions of arty publications.
Fopp, 19 Union St, T0141-285 7190. Good selection of CDs and DVDs at bargain prices.
Good Press Gallery, 12 Kings Court, T0141-552 9458, www.goodpressgallery.co.uk. Part of **Monorail** and **Mono** (see below) this space is dedicated to self-published books, zines, comics, newspapers and art prints. Changing exhibitions where you can pick up interesting prints in limited runs.
Monorail, 12 Kings Court, T0141-552 9458, www.monorailmusic.com. If you are obsessed with all types of music and love vinyl this should be your first port of call. Superb vegan café and adjoining venue Mono stages gigs, all run by the friendly Dep Downie and Glasgow indie band veteran Stephen 'Pastel' McRobbie.
Rubadub, 35 Howard St, T0141-221 9657, www.rubadub.co.uk. Records and music equipment, specializing in dance and electronica for over 20 years.
Waterstones, 153-57 Sauchiehall St, T0843-290 8345. There are 4 floors of books and a basement café at this well-known high street store with a lofty atrium.

Crafts, art and antiques
Glasgow Print Studio Galleries, 103 Trongate, T0141-552 0704, www.gpsart.co.uk. Tue-Sat 1000-1730, Sun 1200-1700. Now part of the cultural hub **Trongate 103**. One of the largest publishers of original prints in the UK. They display and sell etchings, lithographs and screenprints by hundreds of artists including well-known names like Elizabeth Blackadder, Ken Currie, Peter Howson and Adrian Wiszniewski.
Merchant Square, 71-73 Albion St, www.merchantsquareglasgow.com. Mostly bars and restaurants but at the weekend (Sat 1100-1800 and Sun 1200-1800) stalls appear selling crafts, candles, artwork, potions and sweet treats.

Fashion
Cruise, 180 Ingram St, T0141-572 3200, www.cruisefashion.co.uk. Designer fashion boutique from Edinburgh housed in a handsome building.
Mr Ben, Studio 6, Kings Court, Kings St, T0141-553 1936. Mon-Sat 1030-1730. Colourful range of retro clothing. They'll fit you out with jeans, ballgowns and even old nylon Y-fronts.
Urban Outfitters, 157 Buchanan St, T0141-248 9203. Street fashion chain with a retro bent that has branched out into homeware and gifts.
Vivienne Westwood, Unit 3 Princes Sq, T0141-222 2641. British fashion icon known for an eclectic mix of tartan, bondage, punk and theatricality.

Markets
The Barras, London Rd. Sat, Sun 0900-1700. This is Glasgow's famous East End market with over 1000 traders flogging their wares. Worth coming if only to hear their patter.

Outdoor gear
Adventure 1, 38 Dundas St, T0141-353 3788, www.adventure1.co.uk. Outdoor and military surplus gear.
Graham Tiso, 129 Buchanan St, T0141-248 4877. Famous Scottish outdoor shop, which has 5 floors of boots, waterproofs, maps – all the kit you'll need for exploring the hills.

Shopping centres
Buchanan Galleries, T0141-333 9898. Sun 1100-1700. Has a large branch of the **John**

Lewis department store, **East**, **Gap**, **Levi Strauss** and **Mango**.

The Italian Centre, 19 John St, Merchant City, T0141-5522277. Designer fashion emporiums and other upmarket shops, cafés, restaurants.

Princes Square, Buchanan St, T0141-221 0324. Classy Rennie Mackintosh themed shopping centre with an abundance of cafés and eateries to keep you going while you shop. Clothes and shoe shops here include **Vivienne Westwood**, **Cos**, **French Connection** and **Whistles**, and there are beauty shops such as **Arran Aromatics**, **Crabtree and Evelyn**, **Kiehls** and **Space NK**. Olie & Nic for clothes, scents, gifts and jewellery.

St Enoch Centre, Argyle St, T0141-204 3900. Huge mall crammed with all the usual high-street suspects like **Debenhams**, **Boots**, **Topshop**, **H&M** and fast food outlets.

West End *p39, map p40*
Books and music
Fopp, 358 Byres Rd, T0141-337 7490. Another branch of the popular music and media store. Bag a boxset, CD or art-house film at decent prices. It has small selection of vinyl, headphones, music merchandise (band T-shirts etc) and books too.

Voltaire and Rousseau, 12-14 Otago La, T0141-339 1811. An old established antiquarian bookstore and a favourite with students and literary types. Piles of books and its resident cats make V&R a cramped yet beguiling trove for the serendipitous unearthing of a rare tome, dontcha-know.

Fashion
Handbags and Gladrags, 158 Dumbarton Rd, Partick (next to Kelvinhall Underground). Second-hand designer and vintage clothing. Some true finds to be found.

Pink Poodle, 181 Byres Rd, T0141-357 3344, www.lovelaboutique.com. Local fashion designer Tracy Kinnaird is inspired by pin-up girls of the 50s.

Strawberry Fields, 517 Great Western Rd, T0141-339 1121. For bright and cheery children's clothing.

Watermelon, 603 Great Western Rd, T0141-334 3900, glasgowvintage.co.uk. Slightly more upmarket but still affordable vintage clothing for men and women.

Food and drink
Heart Buchanan, Byres Rd, T0141-3347626, www.heartbuchanan.co.uk. Excellent deli with lots of fresh sandwiches and cakes. They specialize in restaurant quality take-home meals to reheat – there's a veggie meal each day.

Peckham's, 124 Byres Rd, T0141-357 1454, www.peckhams.co.uk. Reliable outlet stocking fine wines and all sorts of scrummy foods for posh picnics and treats. Also at a handsome building in the Merchant City on 61-65 Glassford St, with a smart café.

Home and gifts
Boxwood, 388 Byres Rd, T0141-357 6642, boxwood.net. Homeware for the lover of shabby chic or Scandi cool.

Damselfly and the Queen Bee, 380 Great Western Rd, T0141-314 0119, www.damselflycrafts.com. Vintage-inspired stuff for the modern day dandy.

Galletly and Tubbs Interiors, 439 Great Western Rd, T0141-357 1001, www.galletlytubbs.com. Homeware, sometimes with an Eastern touch, also ceramics, soft furnishings and jewellery.

Nancy Smillie, 53 Cresswell St, Byres Rd, T0141-334 4240, www.nancysmillieshop.com. This graduate of the **Glasgow School of Art** knows a thing of beauty when she sees it. For glass, ceramics, soft furnishings, lighting and trinketure.

Timorous Beasties, 384 Great Western Rd, T0141-337 2622, www.timorousbeasties.com. Their famous fabric and wall paper designs include birds, insects, clouds, multi-stories and vagrants (the 'Glasgow Toile') and are sought after by some of the swankiest hotels.

Vintage and antiques
Circa Vintage, 37 Ruthven Lane, T0141-334 6660, www.circavintage.co.uk. Down cobbled lane off Byres Rd, Circa spans the decades with intriguing threads, jewellery and curios.

De Courcy's Arcade, 5-21 Cresswell La, T0141 334 6673. A cluster of shops selling all sorts of antiques from art deco treasures to 20th-century bric-a-brac. It's a trip down dusty memory lane and the shop owners are often game for barter and some banter.

Starry Starry Night, 19 Dowanside La, T0141-3371837, www.starrystarrynight vintage.co.uk. This place will bring a smile to your face for its range of old and vintage clothes from the 1980s back to Victorian times.

Southside *p49, map p26*
Fashion
Butterfly Kisses, 8 Skirving St, Shawlands, T0141-649 3552. Unusual lesser known designers as well as gifts and homeware.

Home and gifts
Pierrot et Coco, 3 Abbot St, Shawlands, T0141-649 2489, www.pierrotetcoco.com. From candles, to loose tea, to art books. All necessities rather than luxuries.

Slaters, 165 Howard St, T0141-552 7171, www.slaters.co.uk. A famous Glasgow institution of 30 years vintage selling menswear and womenswear.

Food and drink
Ian Mellis, 492 Great Western Rd, T0141-339 8998, www.mellischeese.net. Wonderful cheese shop full of unusual varieties of cheese ranging from strong blues, to creamy bries. Great range of Scottish cheeses like Isle of Mull Cheddar or Criffel, a soft cheese, and plenty of Irish cheeses too, such as the unusual Coolea.

○ What to do

Glasgow *p20, maps p22, p26, p40 and p42*
Boat trips
Clyde Cruises, Victoria Harbour, Greenock, T01475-721 281, www.clydecruises.com. Runs 6 routes along the Clyde including the popular circular City Cruise that departs Braehead, takes in the Science Centre, Riverside Museum and City Centre Pontoon before returning to Braehead. It costs £12/concession £6 for a **Day Explorer** ticket. Other trips take in the Titan Crane and distillery at Clydebank; Doon the Water to Dumbarton Rock (£15/concession £8); and the seasonal Govan to Riverside Museum ferry (£3/concession £2).

Clyde Link, T0871-705 0888, www.clydelink. co.uk. This company currently runs the Renfrew-Yoker ferry.

Seaforce, T0141-2211070, www.seaforce. co.uk. Trips from late-Feb to late-Oct must be booked. Based on the **Tall Ship** next to the **Riverside Museum**, this company offers high-speed powerboat trips along the Clyde. Trips range from a 20-min 'taster' (£12 or concession £6) to a 4-hr trip to the village of Kilcreggan (includes a chance to visit the village), costs £50, concession £35. The most popular trip goes to the volcanic plug of Dumbarton Rock, which is £22 or concession £16.

The Waverley, 36 Lancefield Quay, T0845-130 4647, www.waverleyexcursions.co.uk. Sailings take place from Easter to Sep. Trips range from £10-30. With a home mooring at Anderston Quay, east of the **Science Centre**, the Waverley is the world's last ocean-going paddle steamer. It's one of a former fleet of pleasure boats that used to take Glaswegians on trips 'doon the watter' to Clyde coast resorts. After a £6 million refit and restoration to her original glory she is much in demand, with trips around the UK. The operator's other ship is the 1949-built *Balmoral*. You can take still take day trips on the *Waverley* along the Clyde to Dunnoon, Largs, the Kyles of Bute and Arran, etc.

There are further excursions to Oban, Skye, Knoydart and Iona. The return trip from the Glasgow Science Centre to Dunoon costs £29/children £14.50. Check the website for latest schedule and book online.

Bus tours
City Sightseeing Glasgow, T0141-204 0444, www.citysightseeingglasgow.co.uk. Costing £12, concession £10, children £6, family (2 adults, up to 3 children) £26. The complete tour takes in Glasgow Cathedral, Merchant City, People's Palace, Science Centre, Tall Ship, Kelvingrove and the Botanics. It lasts 1 hr 45 mins, although you can hop on and off as you please. Tours leave from George Sq and run every 15-30 mins late Jun-Sep (from 0930-1815 in summer).

Cycling
There are several scenic cycle paths in and around the city, giving the visitor the opportunity to escape the noise and traffic and to stretch their legs. There are also several long-distance cycle routes which start in Glasgow. The tourist office has a wide range of maps and leaflets detailing these routes, which follow quiet back streets, public parks and disused railways for much of the way. Many of the routes start at Bell's Bridge (by the SECC). For the most up-to-date information on the expanding network of cycle routes in the area, and throughout the country, contact **Sustrans**, www.sustrans.org.uk, or www.cyclingscotland.com. For bike hire, see page 83.

The **Clyde Coast Cycle Routes**, run from Bell's Bridge at the SECC through some of the city's parks and closely follows the old Paisley–Ardrossan Canal to Greenock, Gourock and on to Ardrossan, for ferries to the Isle of Arran. It's 28 miles one way as far as Gourock and the route is covered by the Glasgow and Clyde Coast Cycle Routes leaflets, in the Glasgow to Paisley and Paisley to Greenock sections. There is also a Clyde to Forth Cycle Route, a Millennium cycle route that runs between Edinburgh and Gourock.

Glasgow–Loch Lomond Cycle Way, for both walkers and cyclists, runs for 21 miles from the centre of Glasgow, following a disused railway track to Clydebank, the Forth and Clyde Canal towpath to Bowling, then a disused railway to Dumbarton, and finally reaching Loch Lomond by way of the River Leven. The route continues all the way to Killin, in the heart of the Perthshire Highlands, via Balloch, Aberfoyle and Callander.

Football
The 2 main Glasgow teams are Rangers and Celtic, who regularly attract crowds of over 50,000. The domestic football season runs from Aug to mid-May. Most matches are played on Sat and there are also games during the week on Tue and Wed evenings. Ticket prices start from around £30.

Celtic FC are based at Celtic Park, Parkhead, T0871-226 1888, www.celticfc.net, while their bitter rivals **Rangers FC** are based at Ibrox Stadium, T0871-702 1972, www. rangers.co.uk. The national team plays at Hampden Park, which is also the location of the **National Football Museum**, see page 51. For a less-charged and friendly atmosphere head to Firhill Park in the West End, home of **Partick Thistle**, T0871-402 1971, ptfc.co.uk. Adult prices start at £17 while under-16s get in for free.

Golf
There are many municipal courses in and around Glasgow, as well as several top-class championship courses within easy reach of the city. Green fees will often cost from £40 upwards. Among the courses are:
Haggs Castle, 70 Dumbreck Rd. Visitors Mon-Fri. An 18-hole course.
Knightswood Golf Course, Lincoln Av, T0141-959 6358. A 9-hole course.
Lethamhill Golf course, 1240 Cumbernauld Rd, T0141-770 6220, www.glasgow.gov.uk. 18 holes.

Loch Lomond, Luss, T01436-860223, www.lochlomond.com.
Prestwick, Prestwick, T01292-477404, www.prestwickgc.co.uk.
Royal Troon, Troon, T01292-311555, www.royaltroon.co.uk.
Turnberry, Ayrshire, T01655-331000, www.turnberry.co.uk.
World of Golf centre, 2700 Great Western Rd, Clydebank, T0141-944 4141, www.worldofgolf-uk.co.uk. Has a large driving range and a teaching academy.

Taxi tours
Glasgow Taxis, T0141-429 7070, www.glasgowtaxisltd.co.uk. Glasgow taxi drivers are known for their patter and in-depth knowledge of the city, so a taxi tour is an option worth considering. City tours last 1 hr and take you round all the main places of interest, £25 per taxi (maximum 5 passengers), available 24 hrs. There's also a 2-hr tour, which also takes you past Southside attractions like Scotland St School Museum, House for an Art Lover and the Burrell Collection (where you can finish the tour if you choose), £45 per taxi. Pick-ups can be at any point on the route.

Walking tours
Spirit of Glasgow, www.spiritofglasgow.co.uk. From £12. Horror walks and themed history walks, including Murder Mystery adventures. The Horror Walk starts at the Glasgow Cathedral Precinct at 2100 and takes in the Necropolis.

⊖ Transport

Glasgow *p20, maps p22, p26, p40 and p42*
Air
Glasgow International airport is the main departure point in Scotland for flights to North America. There are also regular flights to several European destinations and many domestic flights. There are also flights to Glasgow Prestwick. See also page 7.

Airlines include: **Aer Lingus**, T0845-084 4777, www.aerlingus.com; **BMI Baby**, T0870-264 2229, www.bmibaby.com; **British Airways**, T08457-733377, www.britishairways.com; **easyJet**, T0870-600 0000, www.easyjet.com; **Emirates**, T0870-243 2222, www.emirates. com/uk; **Fly Be**, T0870-567 6676; **Icelandair**, T0845-758 1111, www.icelandair.com; **KLM**, T0870-507 4047, www.klm.com.

Bus
For short trips in the city fares are £1.20, all-day tickets £4. On most buses you'll need to have exact change. After midnight till 0400, there's a limited night bus service (more frequent at weekends). A good way to get around town is to buy a ticket for one of the guided bus tours; see box, page 9.

For longer journeys, **Scottish Citylink**, T08705-505050, www.citylink.co.uk, runs services to most major towns in Scotland. There are buses to **Edinburgh** every 20 mins (1¼ hrs); half hourly buses to **Stirling** (45 mins) and hourly to **Inverness** (4 hrs); 13 buses daily to **Aberdeen** (4 hrs); 3 daily to **Oban** (3 hrs); 4 daily to **Fort William** (3 hrs); 3 daily to **Portree** (7 hrs); and half hourly to **Perth** (1½ hrs) and **Dundee** (2¼ hrs). First Glasgow (T0141-423 6600, www.firstgroup.com) runs buses to **Milngavie**, at the start of the West Highland Way (40 mins).

Car hire
Arnold Clark, 188 Castlebank St, T0141-339 98861 (also at the airport, T0141-848 0202), www.arnoldclark.com. **Avis**, 70 Lancefield St, T0141-221 2877 (also at the airport, T0141-887 2261), www.avis.co.uk. **Enterprise**, 45 Finnieston St, Unit 4, T0141-221 2124, www.enterprise.com. **Hertz**, 138 Hydepark St, T0141-248 7736 (also at the airport, T0141-887 7845), www.hertz.co.uk.

Cycle hire
See page 9 for bike hire companies. For details of cycle routes, see page 82.

Taxi

There are taxi ranks at Central and Queen St train stations and Buchanan bus station. To call a cab, try **Glasgow Taxis**, T0141-429 7070, glasgowtaxis.co.uk, who also run city tours; see page 83. Minimum fare around the city centre is £2.40. To the Burrell collection from the city centre (about 3 miles) should cost around £12.

Train

Trains leave from Glasgow Central mainline station to all destinations south of the Clyde, including to **Greenock** (for ferries to Dunoon), **Wemyss Bay** (for ferries to Rothesay), **Ardrossan** (for ferries to Arran) and to Prestwick airport. There's a low-level station below Central station which connects the southeast of the city with the northwest. This cross-city line serves the SECC and a branch runs north to **Milngavie**, at the start of the West Highland Way. There's also a line from Queen St which runs west all the way to **Helensburgh**, via **Partick** and **Dumbarton**. Branches of this line run to **Balloch**, at the south end of **Loch Lomond**, and **Milngavie**.

Scotrail also operates the West Highland line from Queen St north to **Oban** (3 daily, 3 hrs), **Fort William** (3 daily, 3¾ hrs) and **Mallaig** (3 daily, 5¼ hrs). ScotRail also run services to **Edinburgh** (every 15 mins (30 mins between 1900-0700) 50 mins, £7.90 cheap day return), **Perth** (hourly, 1 hr), **Dundee** (hourly, 1 hr 20 mins), **Aberdeen** (hourly, 2½ hrs), **Stirling** (every 30 mins, 30 mins) and **Inverness** (3 daily, 3½ hrs).

Underground

Locals affectionately call it the 'Clockwork Orange', as there's only 1 circular route serving 15 stops and the trains are bright orange. It's easy to use and there's a flat fare of £1.40, or you can buy a Discovery day ticket for £3.80. Trains run roughly every 5-8 mins from approximately 0630 till 2235 Mon-Sat and from 1100 till 1750 on Sun. For latest info consult www.spt.co.uk.

Around Glasgow *p53*
Paisley

There are frequent buses, which stop at the abbey. Buses depart from Gilmour St station every 10 mins for Glasgow Airport, 2 miles north of town. There are frequent trains to Gilmour St station from Glasgow Central.

Firth of Clyde

There are buses every hour from Buchanan bus station and regular trains to **Greenock** from Glasgow Central.

At **Gourock and Wemyss Bay** ferries leave frequently every day on the 20-min crossing. For details call CalMac, T0870-565 0000. **Western Ferries**, T01369-704452, also runs a ferry service (every ½ hr) between **Gourock** and **Dunoon**. They leave from McInroy's point, 2 miles from the train station, from where Citylink buses also depart. **Clyde Marine**, T01475-721281, www.clyde-marine.co.uk, runs a frequent passenger-only ferry service to **Kilcreggan** (10 mins) and a less frequent service (40 mins) to **Helensburgh**, daily. **Clyde Marine** also run cruises on the Firth of Clyde to **Brodick on Arran**, **Tighnabruaich**, or **Tarbert** on Loch Fyne (Jun-Aug). Note that these leave from Victoria Harbour by the station. Trains and buses to Glasgow are the same as for Greenock. Gourock train station is next to the **CalMac** ferry terminal.

To **Dumbarton** there are trains to Dumbarton Central and Dumbarton East stations running regularly from Helensburgh, Balloch, and Glasgow Queen St.

The Clyde Valley

Trains to **Blantyre** leave from Glasgow Central every ½ hr. It's a 20-min journey. Buses run regularly from Buchanan bus station; take nos 63 or 67 for Blantyre and nos 55 or 56 for **Bothwell**.

For **East Kilbride**, take First Bus no 31 from the St Enoch Centre in Glasgow to Stewartfield Way, or a train.

To **Lanark** there are hourly trains from Central station. There's an hourly bus service from Lanark train station to **New Lanark**, but the 20-min walk is recommended for the wonderful views. The last bus back uphill from the village leaves at 1700. To book a taxi, call **Clydewide**, T01555-663813.

ⓘ Directory

Glasgow *p20, maps p22, p26, p40 and p42*
Dentists For dental emergencies go to the Glasgow Dental Hospital, 378 Sauchiehall St, T0141-211 9600.
Hospitals Glasgow Royal Infirmary, 84 Castle St, T0141-211 4000, near the cathedral. Southern General Hospital, Govan Rd, T0141-201 1100, is the main South Side hospital. **Left luggage** There's an office at Buchanan bus station, daily 0630-2230, also lockers at Central and Queen St train stations (£7 per day). **Pharmacies** Superdrug, Central station, T0141-221 8197, Mon-Fri, till 2130, Sat, Sun till 1700. Munroes', 693 Great Western Rd, T0141-339 0012, open daily till 2100. **Police** 945 Argyle St, T0141-532 3200. Free emergency numbers are T999 or T112.

Contents

Footnotes

Background

Architecture

Glasgow's heyday: Thomson and Mackintosh

Glasgow grew phenomenally through the 19th century to become the 'Second City of the Empire'. While acres of tenements housed artisans and middle-class families, earlier Georgian suburbs were abandoned for commodious villas for the prosperous, designed by leading architects in areas like Kelvingrove. Many, especially on the south side, were designed by Alexander 'Greek' Thomson (see box, page 52) using Classical Greece and Egypt as inspiration. The best known of his public works is the Greek Revival church in St Vincent Street (1858). The originality of his work is itself currently enjoying a long-overdue revival.

While Glasgow University (1870) by Gilbert Scott was inspired by medieval Flemish cloth halls, banks were modelled on Renaissance *palazzos*. Thomson designed Egyptian-style warehouses, and Burnet in the 1890s returned from New York to design tall, narrow-fronted buildings with steel frames. By 1896 and Charles Rennie Mackintosh's debut, Glasgow had the most exciting architecture in Europe.

20th century: Traditionalism and modernism

The forward-looking Beaux-Arts rationalism of Burnet and company was challenged by Traditionalists reacting against aggressive modernity and advocating traditional building materials and craftsmanship, and referring back to 16th- and 17th-century vernacular architecture. Rennie Mackintosh was a leading, if independent exponent, as exemplified at Hill House in Helensburgh, while a more mainstream Arts and Crafts aesthetic was adopted by Robert Lorimer who 'restored' many early houses, as well as designing anew. In contrast, art deco was favoured by architects such as Glasgow's Jack Coia and, by the mid-century, Basil Spence was a champion of modernism. Traditionalism versus modernism was to become an enduring theme. Economic depression and dramatic social change brought an urgent need for solutions to both rural depopulation, and urban overpopulation and decay. Already by the 1930s two contrasting visions of social progress were being proposed: restoration of organic unity versus modernist utopia.

Post-war to present day

A desperate need for housing resulted in massive building projects into the 1970s transforming cities. Many historic buildings were demolished and city centres gutted in an effort to remedy post-war dereliction. The first residential tower blocks, the epitome of the Modern Functionalist brave new world, appeared, most notoriously in Glasgow's Gorbals. Urban over-spill was re-housed in New Towns such as Cumbernauld which, although internationally acclaimed in the 1960s, was unpopular with its inhabitants.

Literature

One of the most important 20th-century Scottish novelists is **Robin Jenkins**, referred to as "the Scottish Thomas Hardy". It was Jenkins who put his native city of Glasgow firmly on the literary map. His most Glaswegian of novels, *A Very Scotch Affair* (Gollancz, 1968), is still regarded as a highpoint in pre-1970s Glasgow fiction. Jenkins is also recognized as the founder of new Scottish fiction and a precursor to Kelman and Welsh as portraying an unsentimental view of Scottish life. Among his other novels are *The Cone Gatherers* (MacDonald 1955), *Fergus Lamont* (Edinburgh Canongate 1979) and *Childish Things* (Canongate 2001).

Another Glasgow literary talent of this time is **William McIlvanney**. Though he had already published two Glasgow novels in the 1960s, it was the following decade which saw him emerge as one the city's greats. In *Laidlaw* (Hodder and Stoughton, 1977), McIlvanney explored Glasgow's seedy, criminal underbelly through the eyes of the eponymous police Detective-Inspector, who became as much a part of the city as Ian Rankin's Rebus has become a part of Edinburgh. Two subsequent crime thrillers featuring Laidlaw, *The Papers of Tony Veitch* (Hodder and Stoughton, 1983) and *Strange Loyalties* (Hodder and Stoughton, 1991) helped McIlvanney transcend the crime novel genre, in the same way that Ian Rankin has done today.

If the 1970s were good for the image of Glasgow literature, then the 1980s were nothing short of earth-shattering. In 1981 the totally original debut novel by **Alastair Gray**, *Lanark: A Life in Four Books* (Canongate, 1981), changed everything. It single-handedly raised the profile of Scottish fiction. Suddenly, the outside world stood up and took notice. Since then, Scottish writers have gone from strength to strength, most notably with **James Kelman**, a giant on the literary scene, whose brilliant novel, *How Late It Was, How Late* (Secker and Warburg, 1994), won the Booker Prize. A one-time bus conductor, Kelman is a committed and uncompromising writer whose use of dialect has attracted as much criticism from the literary establishment as it has praise from fellow writers at home. When some reviewers accused him of insulting literature, he retorted that "a fine line can exist between elitism and racism. On matters concerning language and culture the distinction can sometimes cease altogether."

Kelman has revolutionized Scottish fiction by writing not just dialogue but his entire novels in his own accent, and the debt owed to him by young contemporaries is immense. Writers such as Duncan Mclean, Alan Warner and Irvine Welsh all cite Kelman as a major influence on their writing. Cairns Craig, who has written widely on the modern Scottish novel, states that Kelman's real importance lies in his original use of the English language. "He can be seen as a post-colonial writer who has displaced and reformed English in a regional mode". Among Kelman's finest is his first novel, *The Busconductor Hines* (Polygon Books, 1984) and *A Disaffection* (Secker and Warburg, 1989). *Kelman's Translated Accounts* (Secker and Warburg, 2001) was seen as his most 'difficult'. One literary critic claimed that, while it took Kelman three years to write, it might take the reader three years to understand it.

There are many other notable Glasgow novelists who began to make their name from the 1980s onwards. **Jeff Torrington**, the Linwood car-plant shop steward who was discovered by Kelman, won the Whitbread Prize for his debut novel *Swing Hammer Swing* (Secker and Warburg, 1992), which is set in the Gorbals of the late 1960s. **Janice Galloway** received much praise for her first novel, *The Trick is to Keep Breathing* (Vintage, 1990), which was on the shortlist for Whitbread First Novel, and followed it up with an excellent collection of short stories, *Blood* (Secker and Warburg, 1991). Another brilliant collection of mostly Glasgow short stories is **AL Kennedy**'s *Night Geometry and the Garscadden Trains* (Edinburgh: Polygon, 1991), while *So I am Glad* (Jonathan Cape, 1995) is a Glaswegian take on Magic Realism.

The same year that Kelman's debut was published saw the death of one of Glasgow's forgotten literary sons, **Alexander Trocchi**. Born in 1925 to Italian immigrant parents, Trocchi moved to Paris where he rubbed shoulders with the likes of Samuel Beckett, William Burroughs and Alan Ginsberg and published his brilliant and influential debut novel, *Young Adam* (1954), which soon became a beat cult classic and which was made into a film starring Ewan MacGregor, Tilda Swinton and Peter Mullan. Trocchi's initial literary talents were soon diluted by his prodigious drug consumption and he became better known as a counter-culture icon than a literary figure. Nonetheless, he was an inspiration to a new generation of Scottish writers led by Irvine Welsh, who began publishing in magazines such as *Rebel Incin* the early 1990s.

An exponent of the so-called 'tartan noir' genre is **Louise Walsh**, whose much acclaimed debut novel, *The Cutting Room* (Canongate, 2002) explores the dark recesses of Glasgow through the eyes of a gay, middle-aged auctioneer.

Glossary

Auld	old	**Keek**	look furtively
Aye	yes	**Ken**	know
Bairn	child	**Kirk**	church
Ben	hill or mountain	**Lade**	mill stream
Besom	cheeky/rascal	**Laird**	landowner/squire
Blether	to talk nonsense	**Lassie**	girl
Bonny	pretty	**Links**	coastal golf course
Bothy	farm cottage/mountain hut	**Lug**	ear
Brae	hill or slope	**Lum**	chimney
Braw	beautiful	**Mac/Mc**	prefix in Scottish surnames
Breeks	trousers		denoting 'son of'
Brig	bridge	**Machair**	sandy, grassy coastal land
Burn	brook		used for grazing
Canny	careful	**Manse**	vicarage
Ceilidh	social gathering involving	**Merse**	saltmarsh
	singing, dancing and drinking	**Mind**	remember
Clan	tribe bearing same surname	**Muckle**	big
Clearances	evictions of tenant crofters	**Munro**	mountain over 3,000 ft
	by landowners in the	**Neep**	turnip
	Highlands in late 18th and	**Nicht**	night
	early 19th centuries in order	**Nippit**	tight fitting
	to create space for more	**Oxter**	armpit
	profitable sheep	**Partan**	large crab
Close	narrow passage between	**Peely wally**	pale/wan
	buildings	**Pend**	alleyway
Clype	tell-tale	**Pinkie**	little finger
Couthy	cosy	**Poke**	paper bag
Crannog	Celtic lake or bog dwelling	**Provost**	mayor
Croft	small plot of farmland and	**Puddock**	frog
	house	**Reek**	smoke
Cuddie	horse	**Sair**	sore
Doo	dove	**Sassenach**	literally 'southerner' though
Dour	hard/stubborn		commonly used to describe
Dram	small measure of whisky		English
Drouthy	thirsty	**Scunner**	nuisance/disgust
Dunt	bump	**Sept**	branch of clan
Elder	office bearer in Presbyterian	**Shoogle**	shake
	church	**Sleekit**	sly/cunning
Factor	manager of estate/landlord	**Smirr**	fine rain
Firth	estuary	**Sort**	fix/mend
Fash	trouble/bother	**Tattie bogle**	scarecrow
Gallus	cheeky/forward	**Thole**	endure
Ghillie	personal hunting or fishing	**Trauchled**	tired and bothered
	guide	**Wabbit**	exhausted
Glaikit	gormless	**Wean**	child
Girn	moan/whinge	**Wee**	small
Greet	cry	**Wee Frees**	Followers of the Free Church
Haar	sea mist		of Scotland
Hen	dear (female person)	**Wynd**	lane
Howff	traditional pub/haunt	**Yett**	gate or door

Index

Notes